© 2007 CAP/ PIE BOOKS

PIE BOOKS
2-32-4 Minami-Otsuka, Toshima-ku, Tokyo
170-0005 Japan
Tel : 03-5395-4811 Fax : 03-5395-4812
http://www.piebooks.com
e-mail : editor@piebooks.com
     sales@piebooks.com

ISBN978-4-89444-640-3
Printed in Japan

僕は雑誌デザインについて愚直に考え続けてきた。編集という作業の中で、たかがデザインなどと思われたくないからだ。雑誌に歴史があるとすれば、それは雑誌デザインの歴史でもある。では、雑誌デザインとは何か。それを表現する人たちは何を考え、どこへ向かうのか。僕は素朴な疑問を抱えて雑誌デザインに影響を与えたクリエイターのもとを訪ねた。

そしてそこで得た結論は、僕が思っていた「究極の雑誌デザイナーは編集長だ」というような大げさなものではなかった。自分の好きな世界を追求した結果、編集長という立場に行き着いた人、雑誌デザインのかたわらアーティストとしても活動する人などさまざま。また今さらながら雑誌デザインはグラフィックデザインの一分野であり、あらゆる経験と知識を総動員して表現しつつ、今という時代を反映させる瞬発力を必要とするクリエイティブだと感じた。

藤本やすし
アートディレクター

1983年にデザインオフィス「Cap」設立。アートディレクターとして過去に『マリークレール』『流行通信』『olive』『STUDIO VOICE』『Tokion』など、現在では『VOGUE NIPPON』『GQ JAPAN』『GINZA』『BRUTUS』『CASA BRUTUS』を手掛ける。デザイナーとして関わった雑誌は約100誌にのぼる。また、ルイ・ヴィトン、表参道ヒルズの広告印刷物や、アパレルのシーズンカタログなどのアートディレクターも務める。1996年にはgallery ROCKETを原宿にオープン。現在は休廊中だが、2007年秋、南青山にリオープン。2004年3月ギンザグラフィックギャラリーにて「雑誌をデザインする集団CAP展」を開催。著書として、2004年に『雑誌をデザインする集団キャブ』、2006年に『雑誌をデザインする人と現場とセンスの秘密』をピエブックスより発行。
http://www.cap3hats.co.jp

I have been honest to a fault when it comes to magazine design, and this because I don't want it to be thought of as merely design within the job of editing a magazine. If there is a history to be found in magazines, that must be the history of magazine design. So what is magazine design? What are the people who represent the answer to that question thinking, and in what direction are they going? Armed with these simple questions, I visited the creatives who have been influential in the world of magazine design.

And my conclusion, as I suspected, was not a high-flown, definitive statement such as "the ultimate magazine designer is the editor-in-chief". As a consequence of having pursued the things they love, there are people who have achieved the position known as editor-in-chief, and those are active as artists as well as magazine designers; they are all kinds.

What's more, I realized that magazine design is a field within graphic design, and at the same time as mobilizing all your experience and knowledge, it is a form of creativity that requires an instantaneous power that reflects the times in which we now live.
(Fujimoto Yasushi /President, TMDC, Representative director, Cap)

Yashushi Fujimoto
Art Director

Fujimoto worked as an Art Director for many Japanese editorials, such as Marie Claire, Ryuko Tsushin, Olive, Studio Voice and Tokion. Recently, he has been directing for Vogue Nippon, GQ Japan, Ginza, Brutus, and Casa Brutus. He has designed over 100 magazines since he started.
He also has some advertising projects involving Louis Vuitton Japan and Omotesando Hills, as well as several apparel brands.
In 1996, Fujimoto created gallery Rocket, it's a haven for young, progressive artists, photographers, illustrators and designers to display their work in Harajuku. Gallery Rocket is temporarily closed at this moment, but it openes again in Autumn 2007 in Minami Aoyama.
In March of 2004, he created an exhibition at the Ginza Graphic Gallery, called " Cap Magazine Designer's Collective". In addition to this event, he published a book, called " Cap Magazine Designer's Collective". Following this publication, he issued another series of books called, "The

CHRISTOPHE BRUNNQUELL

(Purple)

The arrival of the distinctively different *Purple* had magazines all over the world scrambling to catch up

The last 10 years of magazine design has been the age of *Purple* magazine. The magazine's sense of "*Purple*-ness" is created predominantly by an engaging selection of images, and distinctive yet simple layout. The laid-back, uncomplicated design is an asset that gives the magazine its unique visual style. The equally laid-back Christophe Brunnquell has been working as art director for *Purple* for many years now, since the second issue, and understands more than anyone what the magazine is all about. When we arrived at his atelier in Paris's 18th arrondissement, large work-in-progress paintings, monochrome works influenced by Japanese

yokai (ghosts), were scattered everywhere on the floors and tables in preparation for an upcoming show. With a philosophy more akin to that of an artist than a magazine designer, Christophe brings a superb sense of balance to both his art and magazine work, for example in his positioning of blank spaces. When we asked about his favorite magazines, he mentioned *Celeste*, a magazine from Mexico, which he likes for its savage and experimental style. He also admires Japanese magazine design for combining a sense of tranquility and order with an overload of visual stimulation.

they needed an art director at *Purple*. So I decided to work with them, coming on board as art director in 1993, with their second issue. The first 10 years in particular were full of new challenges, and great fun."

Purple editor Elein Fleiss

Quirky *Purple* editor Elein Fleiss is known for exercising her talents in many aspects of magazine production, not only in her editorial duties, but also for example by taking photographs herself for the fashion pages. Christophe has always enjoyed working with her, as he has been given a lot of freedom as an art director, and they also share similar aesthetic tastes. I suspect being so easygoing has helped keep him in work, and the popularity of *Purple* has also boosted his own popularity.

"At *Purple* I was allowed to be experimental and try out all sorts of things. We changed the format, layout, paper – absolutely everything. I normally worked at Elein's apartment and we would work very closely, discussing things as we went. We have the same taste in everything: photos, graphics, whatever. So when we work, we can work fast and it's really an easy process for us. Elein is very experimental and has a strong vision for things, so I respect her for that. I left *Purple* for a while because I didn't want the magazine, or myself, to get in a rut. I didn't want to become an old actor, like Colombo in the TV series."

New art-focused projects

When we met Christophe, he was working on a book to celebrate the 15th anniversary of *Purple*, working closely with Elein once again. As well as taking on a wide range of commissions in the Parisian fashion industry, such as a supplement for *Figaro*, he has thrown himself enthusiastically into the production of a self-published magazine called *Carnaval* launched in 2004 that mainly showcases his work. He obviously enjoys having absolute creative freedom and developing ideas through drawings and collage.

"Recently, I've been involved in more artistic activities. I still do art direction and design consultancy jobs, but I find the time spent painting the most personally satisfying. In 10 years time, my first job may well be that of artist (laughs)."

Christophe's life-changing encounter with *Purple*

Christophe is a charming character and spoke to us in a relaxed way about his creative endeavors. His first encounter with *Purple* seems to have been due to a series of events and connections, as is often the case, but Christophe's exceptional talent and character were apparent from an early stage in his career.

"I did not go to art school after graduating from high school, but started working as an art director for *Encore* magazine where Sophian Delhomme – the wife of illustrator, Jean-Philippe Delhomme – was working as a director. While I was there, the editors-in-chief of *Purple*, Elein Fleiss and Olivier Zahm came to interview me for the magazine. After the interview, they told me that actually

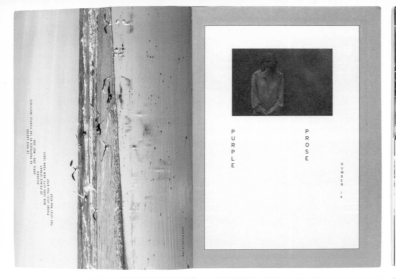

PURPLE PROSE

NUMBER 14

POLYTIX
MAURIZIO CATTELAN

LUNA

CHI PASSA LA LINEA E STRONZO

POLYTIX
JORDAN CRANDALL

02

SQUARES ARE
HUMAN INVENTIONS
by
Marcello Krasilcic

PHOTOGRAPHY CHIKASHI KASAI

PHOTOGRAPHY MARK BORTHWICK

RUN 7   264 CANAL STREET   SERIES 3

PHOTOGRAPHY ANDERS EDSTRÖM
SUSAN CIANCIOLO SUMMER COLLECTION 99, NEW YORK

MODELS SUSAN AND LIZ

SHELLY FOX

NUIT BLANCHE SERIES 3   SERAPH AND SHELLY FOX SUMMER COLLECTION 99, LONDON
                                               PHOTOGRAPHY DONALD CHRISTIE
                                               CONCEPT AND STYLING YOSHIKO SHIOJIRI
                                               MODEL LATIFAH

BALENCIAGA SUMMER COLLECTION 99, PARIS
PHOTOGRAPHY KATJA RAHLWES.
MODEL ANNABEL RUMBLE (SELECT, LONDON)
PHOTO MARC UPSON.

BALENCIAGA MAINTENANT SERIES 13

ORIGINAL GEOMETRY SERIES 13

KOSTAS MURKUDIS

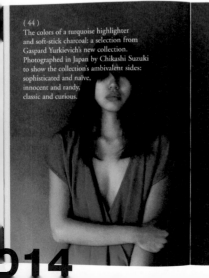

(44)
The colors of a turquoise highlighter
and soft-stick charcoal: a selection from
Gaspard Yurkievich's new collection.
Photographed in Japan by Chikashi Suzuki
to show the collection's ambivalent sides:
sophisticated and naïve,
innocent and randy,
classic and curious.

purple fashion
(53)
SUSAN CIANCIOLO
by / par Marcelo Krasilcic

214

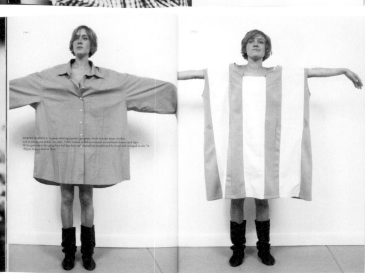

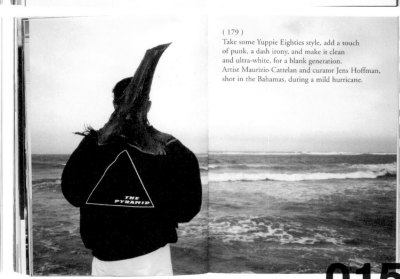

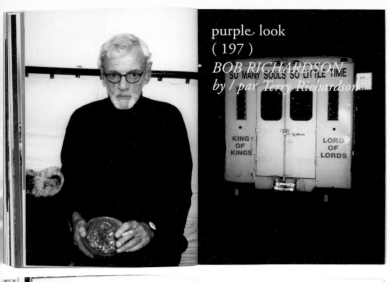

purple prose 18
(256)
ART AND ARTISTS
by / par

Purple asked a number of artists, writers, and musicians to choose a visual artist and to write a short text about him or her. Respondents were given free reign in their choice. The idea was to publish a personal and entirely subjective selection of artists, so that there would be no link to history or to any kind of theme. These may not be the 37 most famous or most important artists in your world, but they all, somehow, exist "specially" in the minds of these writers.

For each artist Pierre Leguillon selected slides, catalogs, magazines, and diverse documentation and rephotographed them so that his photographs would accompany the texts like a "hypertext" picture of pictures. Leguillon usually photographs art in a "live" situation, with people, in architecture, in various sites, which is to say in real life. Here he rephotographed art as it is usually reproduced and gave art reproduction a different twist.

purple prose
(274)
FRANZ ACKERMANN
by / par Joshua Decter

To reinvent the known world we produce maps of world art to be experienced. Mental mapping — the creation of a territory that may have its basis in the real — inevitably breaks down into multiple worlds of imagined geography and a thousand stories of possible bearings.

How to trace the contours of interface between imagination and place?

What is a map if not a demarcation of the self in relation to a location, or a network of locations? Mapping is a procedure at once instinctual and rational, intellectual and intuitive. In order to inhabit the world yet to be known, we invent a new map. But this may have nothing to do with "order" in the traditional, empirical sense.

To reiterate years there has been considerable discussion about the artist as a migratory cruiser, constantly shifting from one context to another, moving across boundaries, dipping in and out of identifiable political and cultural affiliations, reinventing identity positions.

Franz Ackermann is a Berlin-based artist who spends much of his time journeying through various parts of the world. He is, in a sense, based in the world. Yet Ackermann also inhabits the territory of the mind, and he would like to articulate the simultaneity of having one foot in the "actual" world and one foot in the "actual" world of imagination.

Ackermann does not consider himself a tourist, but rather a wanderer who collects sensations from unfamiliar social, cultural territories. These sensations, mutated through the act of recollection, are brought together in the process of developing a visual language that transcends the predictable interplay between representation and abstraction.

Ackermann has always been fascinated with cities and related zones of social organization and how distinct societies construct fixed space through systems of architecture and urban planning. He has traveled extensively in Asia and South America and more recently the Middle East. His art is always, in one intent or another, influenced by the absorption of their influences; drawings are produced during the course of these trips, reflecting an accumulation of lived experiences.

Rather than offering empirical charting of specific architectural styles and/or urban networks, Ackermann's drawings suggest a hybridization of source materials and references. The artist's drawing function like souvenirs of the memory's engagement with place.

So, if Ackermann practices a quirky kind of cultural geography in his works, we might see his tourist tendencies as filtered through the unpredictable mess of intuition and imagination, and vice-versa. A wonderful jumble of proposed relations, and impossibly linked, recollected geographies.

His subjective "maps" (which are not maps in any traditional sense) aggressively decompose the rational order usually associated with designed suburban spaces, willfully corroding the representational pretzel of topographical systems. All of this may indeed have been an effort to obstruct any sort of stable absurdist position — to proclaim "aliènied" as something that is entirely contingent and fluid, or just plain fugitive. Ackermann is able to assess the character of a location — or transitory dwelling — by accentuating the psychological interplay between perception and place.

Collapsing together inscrutability and legibility, Ackermann playfully unravels reference and denotation, suggesting a continuous movement between inscription and erasure, memory and inversion, meaning, and the erasure of meaning.

Franz Ackermann, *Songline*, 1998.
mixed media, installation view

China Art Objects Galleries is a collective gallery, project space
founded by Amy Yao, Steve Hanson, Giovanni Intra, Mark Heffernan,
and Peter Kim. It is located at 933 Chung King Road in Chinatown, Los Angeles.
The project started over the spring of 1998.
It has been officially opened since January 1999.
The gallery space was designed by Pae White.

The artists we have worked with or are working with are:
Pae White, Sharon Lockhart, George Porcari, Jorge Pardo, Bob Weber, Christiana Glidden,
Pae Wesley, Andy Alexander, Daniel Molena, Bako Neri, Kim Fisher, Rebecca Quaytman,
Jennifer Moon, Frances Stark, Scott Reeder, Laura Owens.
With events and performances by:
Steve Prina, Mia Del Toddi, Stephanie Taylor, Mike Kelley.

PARIS
SHARON WAUCHOB'S
BY ANGE LECCIA
STYLE BY SARAH
MODEL SABATINA

FIRST COLLECTION

PARIS
GASPARD YURKIEVICH
FIRST COLLECTION
BY MARTIN LAPORTE
STYLING K'TI LANGEROME
HAIR & MAKE-UP ED & ALEX
MODEL SVETA (VIVA)

NEW YO RK

SUSAN CIANCIOLO WINTER 98-99
BY LAETITIA BENAT

MODELS
ELEIN FLEISS & RITA ACKERMANN

NEW YORK
HELMUT
LANG

BY
RICHARD
PRINCE

CONCEPT OLIVIER ZAHM STYLING MELANIE WARD
THANKS TO DIKE BLAIR

NEW YORK BRUCE WINTER COLLECTION 98/99 BY ALEX ANTITCH

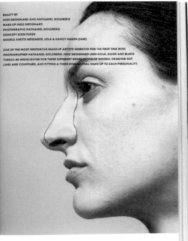

AMSTERDAM

BEAUTY

BEAUTY BY
INGE GROGNARD AND NATHANIEL GOLDBERG
MAKE-UP INGE GROGNARD
PHOTOGRAPHS NATHANIEL GOLDBERG
CONCEPT ELEIN FLEISS
MODELS ANETTE MESSAGER, LOLA & NANCY HAGEN (PAM)

ONE OF THE MOST INNOVATIVE MAKE-UP ARTISTS WORKING FOR THE FIRST TIME WITH
PHOTOGRAPHER NATHANIEL GOLDBERG. INGE GROGNARD USES GOLD, SILVER AND BLACK
THREAD AS HIGHLIGHTER FOR THREE DIFFERENT GENERATIONS OF WOMEN, DRAWING OUT
LINES AND CONTOURS, AND FITTING A THREE-DIMENSIONAL MAKE-UP TO EACH PERSONALITY.

BEAUTY BY
BERNADETTE VAN-HUY AND KATJA RAHWES

PHOTOGRAPHS KATJA RAHWES
MAKE-UP BERNADETTE VAN-HUY
MODEL PAMELA AICH (IMG)
HAIR PIECE KEVIN WOON
GRAY SUEDE JACKET BRUCE
PRINTS MARC UPSON
BEAUTY PRODUCTS MAC

HELMUT LANG, WINTER

A LAYOUT OF COMME DES GARÇONS WINTER COLLECTION

Stereo² collection

Stereo² combining

A combination form meaning "solid"

018

Jonathan Ive
Interview with Dike Blair

1998. —Bondi Blue

Jonathan Ive heads up Apple's design team and is responsible for the look of the iMac (and Bondi Blue) and of Apple's newest line of computers. Since Steve Jobs returned to the company last year, Apple has pruned the corporate tree, disenfranchised their clone makers and concentrated their efforts in three areas where they have excelled: professional computing (especially multimedia and graphics), notebooks and user-friendly desktops.

He and his department figures highly in Jobs' desire and approach to putting Apple back on its original, innovative track. From Ive's bio:

Prior to joining Apple in 1992, 31-year-old, London-born, Jonathan Ive was a partner in the London-based design group Tangerine, which he helped bring to international prominence, amassing clients that included some of the largest manufacturing corporations and most sophisticated users of design in Europe, North America, Japan and Korea.

As the Apple account director at Tangerine he produced a range of design studies in 1991, contributing to the PowerBook development.

Ive's broad-ranging design includes ceramic ware, televisions, VCRs, pens, hair combs, etc. He has been widely exhibited and published at design centers and museums of modern art throughout the US and Europe, receiving many awards.

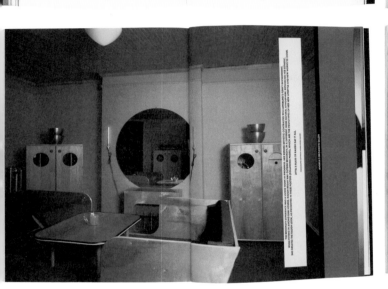

** IT'S ABOUT LOVE **

maurizio cattelan

purple fashion
(59)
JUNYA WATANABE
LIGHT AND AIR

by / par Lars Botten

Shot in the fjords of Norway, Junya Watanabe's voluminous, billowing, polyester evening flowers recall virtual winter web soft, synthetic fabrics that simulate feathery algae, silk cocoons, reindeer moss, the fragile inflorescence of hydrangea.
STYLING YASSMINE ESLAMI
MODEL KATE ELSON
PHOTOGRAPHER'S ASSISTANT BØRGE

purple look
(216)
BRIDESMAIDS
THE MARRIAGE OF MARY WILLS AND BOWMAN KELLEY

by / par Alex Antitch

Memphis, Elvis country. Down-home blues. Line dances. Chitlings. Barbecue. Love in the backseat. A place where tradition and ritual costume, even as the recipes are newer. Frills are out. Tattoos are in. And New York chic is the best ticket for fancy gussying up.
THE WOODRUFF-FONTAINE HOUSE, MEMPHIS, TENNESSEE
FROM LEFT TO RIGHT ZOE JOBRIGHT, FRANCESCA ROMEO, HELEN PARK, GLYNNIS MC DARIS, MINDY WYATT, CATHERINE GREENWOOD, LAURA ARNOLD

purple look
(224)
SCHOOL DAYS
RULE DAYS

by / par Johnny Gembitsky

Sportswear for fast social integration, for an age of dressing down, of hanging out, of group living, group thinking, group togetherness, for a new norm, for a way of life and a time of comfort. A utopia of emptiness.
STYLING SOPHIA NEOPHITOU
MODELS FROM STOKE NEWINGTON SCHOOL, CLISSOLD ROAD, N16
PHOTOGRAPHER'S ASSISTANT VANESSA FRANKLIN
STYLIST'S ASSISTANT BETH DADSWELL
SPECIAL THANKS TO ALL AT STOKE NEWINGTON SCHOOL

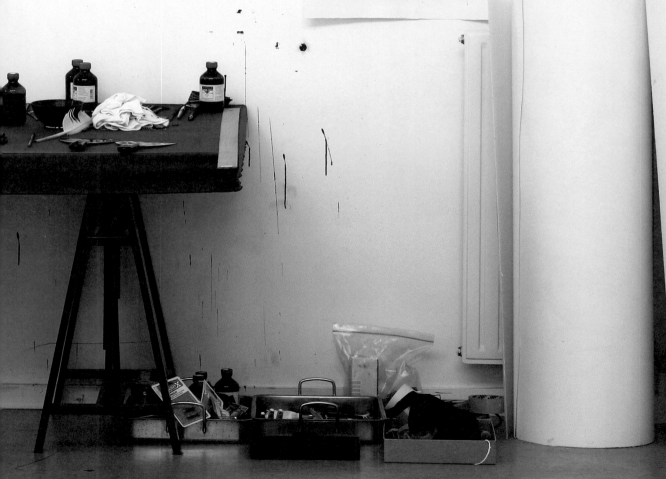

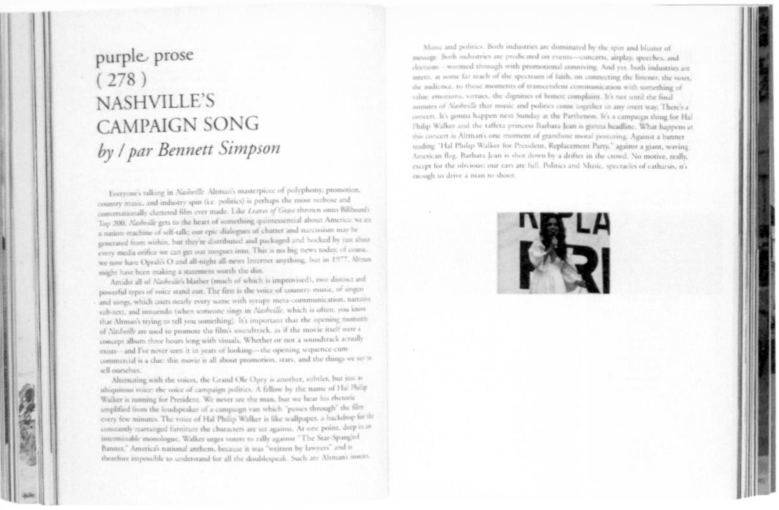

Spread 1 (top left)

purple prose
(278)

NASHVILLE'S
CAMPAIGN SONG

by / par Bennett Simpson

[body text in small print, largely illegible]

Spread 2 (top right)

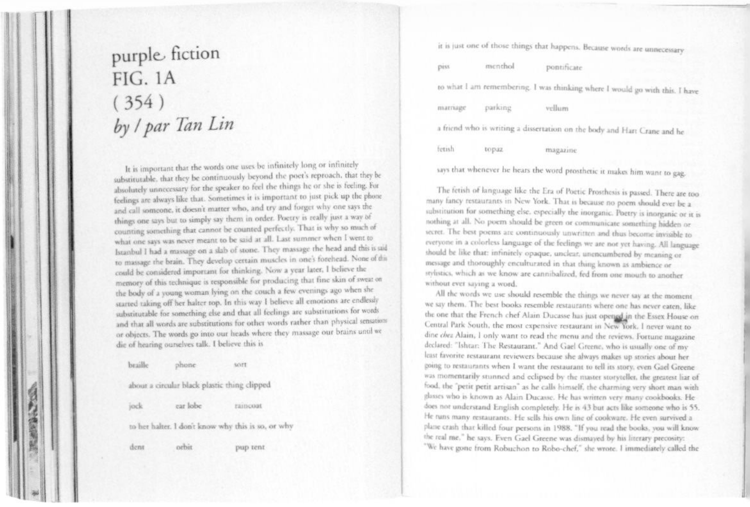

purple fiction
FIG. 1A
(354)

by / par Tan Lin

It is important that the words one uses be infinitely long or infinitely substitutable, that they be continuously beyond the poet's reproach, that they be absolutely unnecessary for the speaker to feel the things he or she is feeling. For feelings are always like that. Sometimes it is important to just pick up the phone and call someone, it doesn't matter who, and try and forget why one says the things one says but to simply say them in order. Poetry is really just a way of counting something that cannot be counted perfectly. That is why so much of what one says was never meant to be said at all. Last summer when I went to Istanbul I had a massage on a slab of stone. They massage the head and this is said to massage the brain...

braille   phone   sort

about a circular black plastic thing clipped

jock   ear lobe   raincoat

to her halter. I don't know why this is so, or why

dent   orbit   pup tent

Spread 3

purple fiction
(404)

NOWHERE AT
THE SAME TIME

by / par James Gooding

Spread 4 (left)

purple fiction
(420)

SCREEN PSYCHOLOGY

by / par Elein Fleiss

Spread 5 (right)

purple fiction
(428)

LOOKING IN LOOKING AT

by / par Henry Roy

Spread 6 (bottom left)

CINDY, 28,
CHRIST CHURCH LUTHERAN ELCA,
SEPTEMBER 17, 1997

CRISTINA, 30,
CATHOLIC CENTER AT NEW YORK UNIVERSITY
(HOLY TRINITY CHAPEL), SEPTEMBER 22, 1997

Spread 7 (bottom right)

P.SEX©ORO ART™

4
LUCY

PICTURES BY RICHARD KERN
GLASGOW, IRELAND

1

VB 36

PERFORMANCE 1998
GALERIE FÜR ZEITGENÖSSISCHE KUNST
LEIPZIG
©VANESSA BEECROFT
1993/215 PURPLE PUBLISHING

**EAST GOES WEST, FUSION,
BARE WALLS,**

12

THE PURPLE GIRL

SABINE BY KATJA RAHLWES
1993/215 PURPLE PUBLISHING

14

hummer

PICTURES BY JAMIL GS
SYLING JASON FARRER
MAKE UP CAROLINA GONZALES
MODEL MELIDA
1993/215 PURPLE PUBLISHING

**POWER HARDWARE,
ULTRA SOFTWARE,**

SELFRIDGES

PHOTOS ANDERS EDSTRÖM
STYLE YOSHIKO SHINZHU
MODEL REKV
TEXT JEFF RIAN

ACTRESS COLLIER SCHORR PHOTO NIAD

RAF SIMONS BY
ANNE–IRIS GUYONNET
STYLE BY DONATIEN VEISMANN
A heraldic device worn and bred like a middle name——
a subtext of who you are, where you are from——
a diacritical slash on your figure, that maybe you wore once but didn't forget——
because it clings like your scent and traces
a part of a profile that follows you through time.

ORIGINAL IMAGE FROM PURPLE FASHION #3

CLOTHES
COMME DES GARÇONS
FOR SUMMER 1997

REDESIGNED BY
PASCALE GATZEN

PHOTO
MARK BORTHWICK

HOW TO WEAR A PICTURE,
REMODELED AND REFORMED SO THAT IT'S NOT IN EVERY SENSE.
WHAT THE OTHER WAS, BUT HOW IT APPEARED IN FLATLAND, IN 2-D,
WITH ITS SHIMMERS AND GATHERS AND SHAPES REFLECTED INTO NEW SHAPE,
THEN REMADE AND REGATHERED AS A SIMULACRUM OF A PICTURE.
PASCALE GATZEN TURNS A PHOTOGRAPH'S RELUCTANT ABSTRACTNESS
INTO ANOTHER DIMENSION. WEARABLE AGAIN, BUT DRAWN AND CUT
FROM AN IMAGE.

ZUCKERZEIT
PERFORMANCE BY JUDY ELKAN
CLOTHES SUSAN CIANCIOLO
PHOTOS BANU CENNETOGLU

F

FILLE #1

PHOTOS
MAURICIO GUILLEN
MODEL / STYLE NASARY MORRIS

SOMETIMES IT TAKES ANOTHER PERSPECTIVE, ANOTHER SET OF CLOTHES
ANOTHER SET OF ROOTS AND EYES TO TURN UP A DIFFERENT EVERYDAYNESS
MEXICO, FRANCE, NEW YORK, GUILLEN'S JOSE GAUCHE–LATIN.

GREENPOINT ASSISTED READYMADES, FASHION PLATE SPECIALS
SILKY AND SMILES WITHOUT ATTITUDE, ANTI–HIP COOL
THE GIRL WALKING DOWN THE STREET IN FRONT OF ROW HOUSES
AND CHAIN–LINK AND NOT FAR FROM SCHOOL
AND PUTTING HERSELF ON THE WAY SHE FEELS IT

OR THE WAY SHE FEELS IN CAMOUFLAGE WEARING SOFT
ANTENNAE, IN A ROOM WITH AN INFLATABLE BUGS THAT JEFF KOONS
MIGHT HAVE POLISHED INTO CHROME AND GRANDMA MOSES WOULD
HAVE THOUGHT OTHERWORLDLY, SITTING WHERE IT SAT, UNDER AN
INDUSTRIAL LAMPSHADE ON A SMALL FLAT ON THE EDGE OF AMERICA

FILLE #2

PHOTOS MAURICIO GUILLEN
MODEL SUE DE-BEER

FILLE #3

PHOTOS MAURICIO GUILLEN
MODEL CARLA

. . . AND THEN HOME, ON THEN OFF.
ELEVATOR UP, SUBWAY DOWN, A DRINK
AND A MEMORY . . .
ALONE AGAIN.

STILL LIFE
MARCH 05
THE DEHUMANIZING ASPECTS OF CULTURE CREATED
AND ITS USE OF THE ADVERTISING, COSMETICS
AND FASHION INDUSTRIES TO EMPHASIZE LUXURY
PARALLELS BETWEEN THE IMMORTALITY OF VANITIES AND THE IMMORTALITY CREATED
IN ADVERTISING AND THE MEDIA AT LARGE THE INFLUENCE OF RELIGION ON CINEMA:
IN THE GREENVILLE OF THE CENTURY, IN HORROR AND VAMPIRE MOVIES
ART DECO AND FILM NOIR REFLECTED THE SENSE BEAUTY AND MURKY ATMOSPHERE
OF THE PERIOD PRINTS RECALL '30S AND '40S FILM COMPANY EMBLEMS

CAFETERIA
MARCH 04
CARTESIAN INFLUENCES ON NATIONALISM
FRAGMENTATION AS AN ESSENCE OF WAR
THE ANONYMOUS BODY WITHIN THE WAR
THE DEAD REPRESENTED BY DOCUMENTS
SERIES OF PAPER GARMENTS
AERIAL SIGNS ILLUSTRATING BODIES RETURNING TO THEIR PLACES OF ORIGIN

HUSSEIN CHALAYAN'S COLLECTION
THEORIES 1994–97
PHOTO MARK BORTHWICK
STYLE JANE HOWE
CONCEPT JANE HOWE / OLIVIER ZAHM

TAKING NAMES

IF YOU'RE EVER ARRESTED, YOUR NAME IS WRITTEN DOWN, YOUR IDENTITY IS TAKEN OVER—
NUMBED, LIKE A FOOT THAT'S FALLEN ASLEEP, WHEN WRITTEN, A NAME IS GIVEN A DIFFERENT
LIFE. IT BECOMES CLASSIFIED. TO RECOVER, TO AWAKEN, OR TO GET OFF THE LIST, IT NEEDS TO BE
MASSAGED. ACCORDING TO EDMUND CARPENTER, "AS LONG AS INFORMATION IS CLASSIFIED—
IN CONTENT, MEDIUM, AUDIENCE—IT'S RESTRICTED AND CONTROLLED. BUT CHANGING ANY ONE
OF THESE THREE DECLASSIFIES IT YOU MAKE IT AVAILABLE FOR NEW CLASSIFICATION.
THAT IS, FOR THE PRODUCTION AND DISTRIBUTION OF NEW KNOWLEDGE."

OK. BUT EVERYTHING IS CLASSIFIED. BEING "GIVEN" A NAME IS A FORM OF NUMBING. THE
WHOLE WORLD HAS BEEN NAMED AND SHELVED BY TYPE AND STYLE, BY CONTENT,
MEDIUM, AND AUDIENCE. CLASSIFICATION IS THE WAY WE GANG UP EVERYTHING SO THAT WE CAN
POSSESS IT—EVEN OURSELVES IN SELF-POSSESSION.

"CONGESTION," ACCORDING TO MARSHALL MCLUHAN, "IS THE INDISPENSABLE PRELUDE
TO GETTING YOUR HAND IN THE OTHER GUY'S POCKET" THEREFORE, TO DECLASSIFY ANYTHING,
IS TO GIVE IT A DIFFERENT LIFE, TO MAKE IT AVAILABLE FOR ANOTHER KIND OF PRODUCTION,
A DIFFERENT USE.

"IT" IS NOT JUST A NAME, IT'S A FORM OF ANESTHESIA, FOR WHOLE FORESTS
OF SLEEPWALKERS.

A MINOR MODE

PHOTOS CAMILLE VIVIER
MODELS
NINA,
DELPHINE,
STEPHANIE

PHOTO ELEIN FLEISS

LEAVING HELSINKI

JEAN-MICHEL
BREAKFAST
AT 6:00 P.M.
PHOTOS
MARK BORTHWICK

235 BERRY STREET

2

Photos **VANESSA BEECROFT MILTOS MANETAS**

BBBB
ACROSS THE EAST RIVER.
SPARSENESS IS THE SENSIBILITY.
NIRVANA OF THE HOME.
GIVING SPACE TO YOUR HEAD.
USE IT TO WORK, AND PUT IT AWAY.
LIE DOWN. STARE AT THE SCREEN.
INTERCONNECT.
ENGAGE TIME ZONES.
ALTER YOUR OWN. MAKE YOUR SPACE
AN OUT-OF-BODY EXPERIENCE.
AN AERIE WHERE YOU CAN AIR
AND CONSIDER AND COPE.
BUT DON'T LET A SPECK REST UNTENDED.

BEDROOM COMMUNITIES. SUBURBS. MUSHROOM TRACTS. ALL GREW OUT OF A NEED FOR ————— INEXPENSIVE HOUSING AND FROM THE AVAILABILITY OF CARS.
IN TURN, THEY BRED SHOPPING MALLS AND FAST FOOD CHAINS. THEY FLOURISHED ALONG WITH ————— THE BABY BOOM GENERATION. TELEVISION.
THE COLD WAR AND NUCLEAR THREAT. IN ESSENCE, THEY ARE SELF-CONTAINED COMMUTER ZONES. ————— WHERE PEOPLE EAT. SLEEP. WATCH TV. BUT ALMOST NEVER WALK.
THEY COME IN UNITS, MADE IN EVERY VARIETY OF STYLE, COLOR, AND SHAPE, AND ARE PROCESSED ————— LIKE THE FOOD, CLOTHING, AND CONVEYANCES THAT TRAFFIC IN AND OUT OF THEM.
THESE ARE MODEL SUBURBS, NESTLED IN WOODS AND DELLS AND BUFFERED WITH PARKS AND ————— COUNTRY CLUBS. AROUND THEM ARE ARRAYS OF STARTER HOMES, AND GRIDS OF
APARTMENT BLOCKS TETHERED BY RAILWAY TRACKS AND SUBWAY LINES, AND RIBBONS ————— OF TARMACADAM TO CONVEY THESE SUBURBANITES TO CITIES OR TO SATELLITE
HUBS CALLED "EDGE CITIES," WHERE MORE PEOPLE WORK THAN LIVE. AT THE EDGE OF CENTERS. ————— COMMUNITIES WITH ARTIFICIAL NAMES LIKE GLENDALE, WESTPORT PLAZA,
CUCAMONGA, WALNUT CREEK. THEY ARE CORPORATE CITIES. THEY SNUGGLE LIKE PUPS ————— AROUND THE CITIES OF THE WORLD, FROM MINNEAPOLIS, TO REYKJAVIK, TO TOKYO,
TO SIDNEY, AND EVEN AROUND PLACES LIKE SAO PAOLO AND BEJING WHERE THEY BREED RIGHT ————— FROM THE DIRT AND SQUALOR. AND WHERE THE GRANDER CORPORATE
SLUGGISHNESS HAS YET ————— TO RIPPLE.

Sleep, Eat, but Don't Walk

sluggish motion.

photos **TAKASHI HOMMA**

The world is but a perennial seesaw....
Even fixedness is nothing but a more
Book 3, Montaigne's Essais

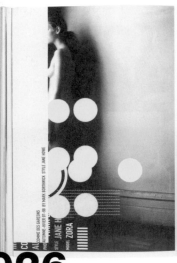

STYLE JANE H
MODEL ZORA
PHOTO AUTOMNE-HIVER 97-98 BY MARK BORTHWICK STYLE JANE HOWE
ALEXANDRE DES GARÇONS
CO

KOJI TATSUNO
PHOTOS BY FRANÇOIS ROTGER
MODEL ESTHER
STYLE ISABELLE PEYRIT
MAKE UP CHRISTINE CORBEL
HAIR DAVID MALLET

INTERVIEW/
SOUND
AND
IMAGE, SELF
AND
PLACE

QUESTIONS...
DIKE BLAIR
ANSWERS...
DOUG AITKEN

DATE...
6/4/97

PLACE...
PARKED CAR IN CHELSEA, NYC

ALPHAWO HOUSE"
RLD

"La construction n'est plus fonctionnelle. Elle n'enjambe aucun abime et ne crée aucun espace habité... elle se suffit à elle-même. Elle est consacrée tout entière à sa propre construction fantasmagorique. Son charme réside bien plus dans l'imprécision de ses limites, dans le caractère indéfini de ses volumes et dans la prédominance du bizarre et de l'accidentel. L'œil se perd dans la perspective sans rencontrer de mur ; tout s'estompe au loin dans une brume bleutée. Parfois le mur se détache du sol pour pénétrer, sous la forme d'une boucle, sans pesanteur, dans l'espace aérien.
Des prismes de verre composent entièrement les panneaux des murs ; derrière ces prismes sont disposés des verres de couleurs. Le jeu d'eau du sous-sol devient une apparition multicolore très agréable grâce à l'astucieuse utilisation de toutes sortes de verre. La fiction de la couleur jaillit du cœur même de la matière. C'est une forme accueillante, ouverte sur le ciel, qui attire l'espace extérieur à la manière d'un miroir ardent. C'est à l'intérieur que l'on prend conscience de l'extérieur et inversement. Il s'agit d'une construction à double espace, d'une abstraction de l'infini."
Cut-up à partir de Simone Rodila, Lubetkin, Bruce Goff, Fredric J.Kiesler, Gropius, Ulrich Conrads et Hans G.Sperlich.
le Nouveau Monde http://www.activeworlds.com

"WIND
OWS

La maison dont la construction a commencé il y a sept ans sur les bords du Lac Washington, près de Seattle. L'état de chantier paraît installé définitivement, et donne à l'extérieur l'aspect incertain et chaotique d'un chantier. Paradoxalement, il s'agit du chantier-laboratoire d'une cyber-house privée conçue comme une sorte de complexe de loisirs ou de parc d'attraction : cinéma, piscine, trampoline). En fait un gigantesque show-room dont l'architecture est entièrement mise au service d'une démonstration télématique, matérialisée par une série de gadgets indiscrets et tyranniques : barrage informatique; code d'accès, mise en mémoire de l'identité et des goûts des visiteurs badgés / *impossible de perdre un invité /* ... les déplacements seront accompagnés par vos musiques et vos images préférées, puisées dans la plus grande collection mondiale d'images numérisées et diffusées sur des écrans omniprésents qui se déclenchent au passage des habitants / la lumière vous précède et le téléphone vous suit partout.
Ma maison offrira des distractions et stimulera la créativité dans une atmosphère détendue, agréable et chaleureuse... Ma maison sait qui vous êtes et si vous vous trouvez... Elle se sert de cette information pour essayer de satisfaire, voir d'anticiper vos désirs... le plus discrètement possible."
la route du futur, Bill Gates, Edition Robert Lafont

OU BIEN... OU BIEN...
BERNARD JOISTEN

Certes, les clichés s'accrochent : la mafia, le sordide sentimental...
Mais le sujet reste en exergue. L'analyse sociale cuit gentiment sous le feu des effets. Du coup, *Goodbye South Goodbye* reste un objet à part.
Tout doucement, le taïwanais Hou Hsiao-Hsien définit une zone d'abstraction cinématographique. L'étonnant travail sur la lumière dégage les situations de toute responsabilité réaliste. Clair-obscur, vert glauque, jaune sable, rouge irradiant des surfaces, chaleur malade, froid ironique, pellicule visible. Suave couleur du saphir oriental...
Autant de climats colorés que de récits.
Voici venu le temps du naturalisme chromatique...
Merci au sens plastique de nous épargner le Message.
Comme dans *Main basse sur la ville* de Francesco Rosi (1963) :
on ne va pas se plaindre du discours, s'il reste en laisse.

INTERVIEW
WITH MILTOS MANETAS

" RIAN...
WHY DO YOU LIKE POWERBOOKS SO MUCH?
MANETAS...
They'e about concentrated power.
HERACLITUS SAID

DEMENTED
IN THE FUTURE-PRESENT

«THE MAN IN THE DARK, LIGHTS A CANDLE FOR HIMSELF WHEN THE LIGHT OF HIS HEAD IS OUT.»

The screen of a PowerBook is that candle .

She walked out of the car into the lot, holding one hand to her purse and the other in a crease of her dress. The clothes moved, but did not fit. Askew. Being dressed made her feel like her body was both transparent, permeable to the light and encoded with significance. A geometry was at work but it had migrated out of the edge of the frame and was now mapped onto the reality of the physical city. The pattern stuck. Every time she walked out of the car into the street, she would check the edge of her clothes. I'm not sure she remembers that motion very time it happens, anymore she is aware of the Puerto-Rican woman sitting in the shade of the building every time she leaves the house on the weekends. No matter how little she notices them, something objective nevertheless makes the reality of their existence into a fact. There is a layer between the clothes and the body, and another which seems to rest as a coat, on top of the garment. Something both public and intimate happens in-between these two layers.

R UN-
RO
ABSTRACTION

SUSAN CIANCIOLO

PHOTOS BY 001

ARI MARCOPOULOS OF JULIANNE CLEAVE,
STORY BY MAI-THU PERRET

@}-->-->--
ANDREAS ANGELIDAKIS
WHERE ARE YOU FROM
PALEBLUE

独特の空気感をまとった『Purple』の登場で
世界中の雑誌が"右へ倣え"になった

　ここ10年くらい、『Purple』の時代が続いている。その空気感は写真選びとレイアウトによるところが大きい。複雑なデザインを施さない、肩の力が抜けたページの繋がりこそ、この雑誌の財産なのだ。2号目から何年間にもわたりアートディレクションを担当しているクリストフ・ブルンケルは、雑誌の気分を十分に理解している。会ってみると彼自身がゆるやかな雰囲気を持つ人物だった。
パリの18区にあるアトリエを訪ねると、個展に向けて制作中の大型ペインティングが所狭しと置かれていた。日本の妖怪に影響を受けたモノクローム作品。雑誌デザイナーというよりアーティストとしての生き方が根底にある彼だが、余白の取り方などバランス感覚は共通するものがある。好きな雑誌はメキシコの『Celeste』。実験的で野性的なスタイルが好きらしい。また、ヴィジュアルを多く扱っても、常に秩序と平静さを失わない日本の雑誌デザインには感心させられる、と彼は言った。

人生を変えた『Purple』との出会い

　日本から来たボクらに、クリストフはなめらかな優しい語り口で、自分の活動について話してくれた。『Purple』との出会いは、どちらかというとよくある偶然の重なりのようだが、働き始めて早々に彼の才能と人格が人並み以上であることが明らかになったようだ。
「僕は高校を卒業してから美術学校などには行かず、すぐに働き出したんです。最初の仕事は、イラストレーター、ジャン・フィリップ・デロームの妻であるソフィアン・デロームがディレクターを務める『Encore』という雑誌のアートディレクション。そこで働いていたときに、創刊時の『Purple』からインタビューを受け、編集長のエレン・フライスとオリヴィエ・ザームに出会いました。インタビューの直後に『実は自分たちもアートディレクターを探しているんだけど……』と誘われて即決したわけです。1993年、2号目からのアートディレクションですね。特に最初の10年間は新しいチャレンジの連続で、とても楽しんで仕事に取り組みました」

編集長エレン・フライスについて

　『Purple』の編集長であるエレン・フライスといえば、編集企画はもちろん、自らファッションページの写真を撮るなど、多様な面で才能を発揮する存在として知られている。同時に、個性派でクセのある人物としても有名だ。ブルンケルはその人柄とセンスのよさからとても気に入られている様子で、デザイン的にもかなりの自由を与えられているという。性格のよさが彼の仕事を長続きさせたし、『Purple』の人気が彼の人気を引き上げたのだとも思う。
　「『Purple』では、判型や紙、レイアウトなど、ありとあらゆるものを変えて、実験的なことをいろいろ試すことができました。この仕事は、エレンのアパートの部屋で作業をすることが多く、いつも話し合いながら進めていました。写真やグラフィックの好みなど、お互いの感性や志向がぴったり合うので、仕事がしやすくて、作業は本当にスムーズ。彼女はいつも新しいことに挑戦しているし、明確なヴィジョンを持っているので、とても尊敬しています。僕が『Purple』から一時期離れたのは、長く続けていくことで、雑誌も自分自身もマンネリ化してしまうのを避けたかったから。TVドラマ「刑事コロンボ」の俳優のようにはなりたくなかったのです」

アートを中心にした新たな活動

　取材時には、再びエレンと密に作業をしながら、『Purple』の15周年を記念するヴィジュアル本のアートディレクションを進めていた。『Figaro』の別冊など、パリのファッション界で幅広く活躍する他、2004年からスタートさせた自身の雑誌『Carnaval』も意欲的に続けている。これは彼のアート作品を中心に掲載した雑誌で、コラージュやイラストなどを思いのままに発表できる、理想的な媒体なのだろう。
　「最近はアート活動がどんどん増えてきています。雑誌のディレクションやデザインコンサルティングの仕事と両立させていますが、自分としては描いているときが一番充実しているかな。10年後には、僕の職業はアーティストになっているかもしれませんね(笑)」

Cristophe Brunnquell

Born 1969 in Neuilly-sur-Seine, France. Brunnquell has been art director of the French fashion and culture magazine *Purple* since 1993. His multifaceted activities also include art direction for Louis Vuitton's 150th anniversary book, Sophie Calle / French Pavilion / 52nd Venice Biennale 2007 and Fashion Guide *Figaro*; design consulting for Fabien Baron and collaborations with Colette, Balenciaga, Céline, Cosmic Wonder, Zucca and others. In 2004 he launched the magazine *Carnaval* in which he prints his own art work, executing every aspect from text to publishing himself. Brunnquell is also famous as an artist.

クリストフ・ブルンケル

1969 年、フランス、ヌイィ・シュル・セーヌ生まれ。1993 年から現在までフランスのファッション & カルチャー雑誌『Purple』のアートディレクターをつとめる。他にも、ルイ・ヴィトン 150 周年記念本や第 52 回ヴェネツィア・ビエンナーレでのソフィ・カルによるフランス館、ファッション雑誌『Figaro』のアートディレクション、ファビアン・バロンのデザインコンサルティング、コレット、バレンシアガ、セリーヌ、コスミックワンダー、ズッカ等ファッションブランドとのコラボレーションなど多方面で活躍中。また 2004 年に雑誌『Carnaval』を創刊。自身のアートワークを掲載しテキストから出版までを自身が行っている。アーティストとしての活動も有名。

DAVID
CARSON
(RAYGUN)

Rebel, yet audience friendly
The act of making the print convey the feel of the era

"People often said I was disrespectful to the writing, but it's absolutely the opposite. If the article was about music, I would listen to the tracks, read the text, interpret and try to draw the reader into it through the page design. I would try to put some emotion into the pages with my layouts – the photographs and illustrations, the typography – and reinforce the feeling of the article."

So explains David Carson, the original art director of the music magazine of the '90s, *RAYGUN*. Being involved from day one, his roles ranged from assigning photo shoots and illustrations, to page design and art direction, a rarity in the often-sectored American magazine world.

"It was a very unusual situation – to have that much freedom. When I finished an issue, I would send it to the printer. Nobody had to OK it. Most of the issues even had different logos. We wanted to give the magazine a feel that was true to the new music of the time. Somebody said, especially with *RAYGUN*, that I was 'experimenting with public'."

Founded in the *Beach Culture*

What led to David's role in the birth of *RAYGUN* was the work he did for *Beach Culture*, which the publisher happened to notice. Over the course of three years starting in 1989, David and one other editor produced but six issues of the West Coast lifestyle magazine, literally in the Southern Californian back warehouse of *Surfer Magazine*.

"Squeezed out of zero budget, I approached every issue of *Beach Culture* as if it was the last. I flew out to California, which I'd left the year before, from New York hearing a rumor of the publication's startup. I'd have worked seven days a week, 24 hours if I could, and I almost did. I was broke, but was really happy doing what I was doing. It's so important to have a venue where you can do what you can do well."

Shifting gears from surfing to editorial design

Pages filled with surfing, skateboard, music, and coastal life: David, who had grown up immersed in the west coast surfing scene, poured his everything into the fruition of *Beach Culture*. From his teenage years David was competing as a professional surfer, and awake or asleep, all he did was surf. It wasn't until he was 26 that he first heard about the field of "graphic design".

"I didn't even know such work existed. I could probably go back to 20 years of surfing magazines, open a page and tell you the caption, but I wasn't looking at them with any special interest in the typography. I happened to get an internship through a friend, and that was my foot in the door. Following the discovery, all the energy that had been going into surfing shifted over to graphic design. But since my college major was sociology, it was more interesting, and still is, for me to take an actual event or music – something that's real – and interpret it, than to design say a product container. Being at a magazine seemed like a natural fit."

David's internship dissolved with the magazine, and he went back to teaching sociology at high school for several years, during which he also participated design workshops in Switzerland. Eventually, *Transworld Skateboard* invited him to join them as an art director, and in 1983 he quit teaching and devoted himself to design for the next the four years. He then accepted an offer to work for *Musician* magazine in New York as a way to break away from being typecast as a surf-skate designer. But with the rumor of *Beach Culture*'s start, David returned again to the West Coast.

RAYGUN and the neck of David Bowie

RAYGUN ran through the '90s, the decade that also bred the grunge music movement. After creating the face and pages for the four years since the magazine's establishment, a friction which led to David's departure arouse...over David Bowie's cover for the 30th issue.

"I had all these pictures of him staring at the camera, and then there was this one...with just his neck. The minute I saw it I new that was the cover. We've all seen split faces, but never this striking. But the publishers happened to be a big fan of Bowie, and they argued that no one would know it was David Bowie. I refused to do the cover, but they put their foot down on this particular occasion, and went with a camera-staring shot. That was really the end. I lost interest, and the publisher didn't assign me the next issue. Had that not been an issue, I would have been there longer but I really felt strongly about that image. To this day, I think 'aargh, it would have been such a great cover!'" He flashes a smile of regret. The neck image ended up on the opening spread. It also appears in David's book, *The End of Print*. The first issue created at the same desk as *Beach Culture*; the second using only the five fonts that came with his rental computer ("That's just a type of thing I would like to allow myself to challenge," says David): all those personal paths reflected into each *RAYGUN* issue. With a shift away from his *RAYGUN*-centric life – listening to the music he acquired for each issue, making a wreck of the office in the creative process – to advertising work, came a new beat: flying down to his Caribbean pad in winter whenever there's a call of a good swell. "When I was a teenager, surfing was all I did and now it came in full circle and I can do it for fun," David grins.

The "End of Print", and beyond

David recently set up a studio in Zurich, where he focuses on advertising, film, and editorial design, but we visited him at his Folly Beach, South Carolina home and office. In early June, at the height of the East Coast's sultry season, the metal mesh covering his front porch was creating curious circles of light, almost like a blow-up of offset print. Added on to the original house by an Austrian architecture student, the relationship between the light and the surface was something akin to David's aesthetics. He suggested what might be similar is that "the work was made to be discovered later; something defined within, besides just the obvious." He described how wonderful it is to read mail and have breakfast in his bright but lightly shaded green backyard, where he also displays his finds from workshop trips around the world, including a handmade sign from Panama, and a layers of posters salvaged from the streets of Brazil, evidence of the way David scours the places he visits.

Neville Brody once looked at *RAYGUN* and exclaimed, "We've gone as far as we can with print...This represents the end of print." David Byrne (former Talking Heads) said, "Print is liberated. It is no longer obligated to simply carry the news." The design revolution in the form of widely distributed music magazine was the source of great praise; it also threatened the traditionalists. One art school even forbade David to set foot on campus in protest. "Love or hate, what I was doing at *RAYGUN* seems to have struck some serious nerves," he quips with smile.

AUTHOR:

PHOTOGRAPHER: [AY]GUNMAGAZINE

INTERVIEWS WITH THE FREAKS

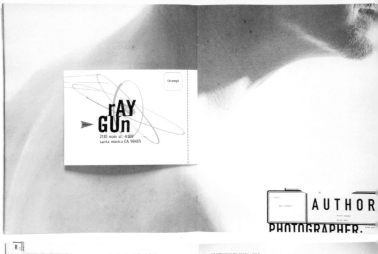

[AY GUn

▶ 2110 main st. #100
santa monica CA 90405

AUTHOR

PHOTOGRAPHER:

QUOTE

by Brian Eno

THOR:
PHER:
[AY]GUNMAGAZINE

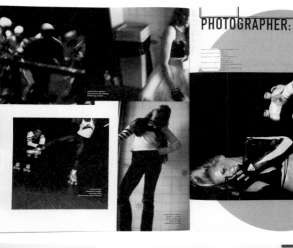

PHOTOGRAPHER:
AGAZINE

PHOTOGRAPHER:

AUTHOR:

QUOTE

[AY]GUNMAGAZINE

03

GUILTY

guilty pleasures

What do the **Jesus** Lizard, Robyn Hitchcock,

Penn Jillette, Ween,

Matthew Sweet,

Bootsy Collins, Ass Ponys,

Orb, Traci **Lords** and others have to call they love?

by Tim Quirk

neil

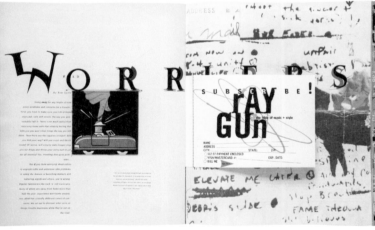

JERRY LEE LEWIS INTERVIEW
BY HENRY ROLLINS

PHOTOGRAPHY BY HUGER FOOTE

Empire of the Sound

A Day in the Life of a Movie · About a Day in the Life of a Record Store

VINYLS

BMPIRE since

WORRIERS

SUBSCRIBE!

RAY GUN
the bible of music + style

NAME
ADDRESS
CITY: STATE: ZIP:
☐ $12.97 PAYMENT ENCLOSED
VISA/MASTERCARD #:   EXP. DATE:
☐ BILL ME

mat thew S we et

photograph Barry Anderson

ICE FUN ON THE ROAD

ACID

PIZZICATO 5IVE
Big*in*Japan
by Aidin Vaziri

'Nuf Said
Isaac Hayes

by Henry Rollins
photography by Melodie McDaniel

m u s i c
b y
d e s i g n :
s h e r r i
o e l l e

DEEP OCEAN, VAST PETE

photography

F1SH-
by doug aiken

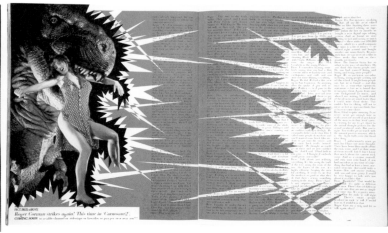

PICTURED ABOVE:
Roger Corman strikes again! This time in 'Carnosaur2'.
COMING SOON to a cable channel or videotape or favorite or pay per view near you!!!

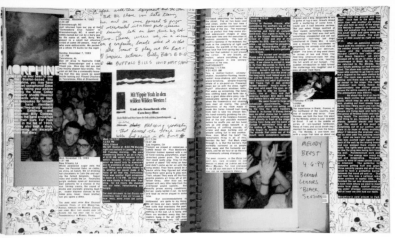

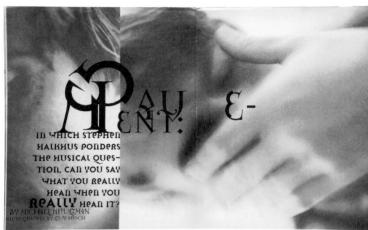

REGAL Affairs
royal trux inter-
view with RICHARDS

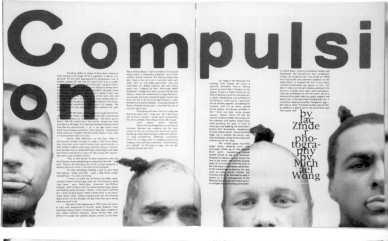

Compulsion

by Jac Zinder
photography by Michael Wong

fashion
spare doll

english middle class women who
wear tons of tacky fake jewelry

April

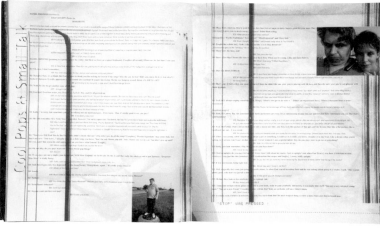

Cool Pops & Small Talk

"STOP" WAS PRESSED

by Matt Diehl Photos

SOMETIMES, man—I don't feel like a
fucking musician,

EXPLOSION
describing the band's typi-
ally savage live
co-guitarist Judah Bauer.

bootsy

Which was kept

#6

DRIPS pieceofiZ

RE-AD

pieceofiZ

I took a calm though congested
30 minute yellow cab ride
uptown from
the Christadora Building at Tompkins Square
to the Michaelangelo Hotel on 51st street
So that
After a cozy little photo session
In the chandelier lobby
and some strategic stalling
what had been scheduled finally was to be
I would interview my friend/mentor
Bob Mould
But all I had on me was
a cheap cassette recorder
and not a single question
Then SERENDIPITY
Bona anytime buddy showed up
lunchtime/writer/commentator etc
Lizz Winstead
& rode elevator with us

BOSTON WAS INDUSTRIAL REAL ESTATE

Boston e

and minimal lo-fi laden grunge licks

SIMMONS   KISS   GENE

STEVE MOON

SUPERCHUNK'S   Mac McCaughan

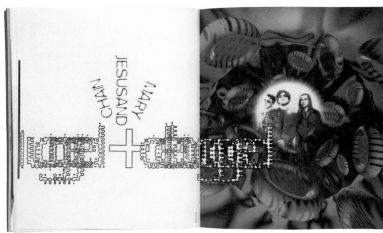

JESUS AND MARY CHAIN

PRETENDERS

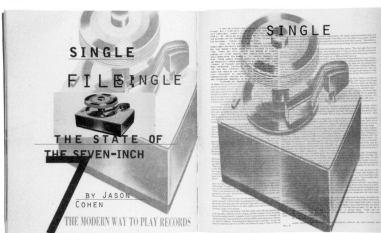

SINGLE

SINGLE

SINGLE

FILE

SINGLE

THE STATE OF
THE SEVEN-INCH

BY JASON
COHEN

THE MODERN WAY TO PLAY RECORDS

CHOICE

CHOICE
ComEs to

pEnsA
colA

CHOiCE

text by L7's Jennifer Finch

forgive
me??

cool
FOR

by Nina Malkin

CATS

Fancy the feline with Robyn Hitchock,
Codeine, Shonen Knife, Cracker,
Therapy?, Killdozer and many more!

SPLIT

joHn
Lyd on

rottEn ito tHE

CorE

helmet

songs in the key of life

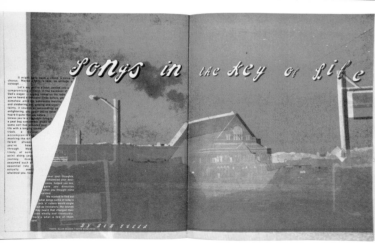

london fashion by carmine day

TANK GIRL★

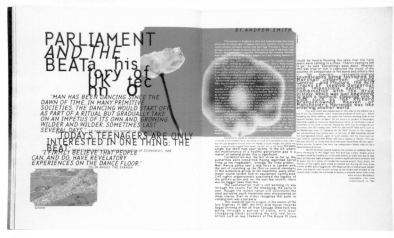

PARLIAMENT AND THE BEAT a his tory of k n tec

BY ANDREW SMITH

"MAN HAS BEEN DANCING SINCE THE DAWN OF TIME. IN MANY PRIMITIVE SOCIETIES, THE DANCING WOULD START OFF AS PART OF A RITUAL BUT GRADUALLY TAKE ON AN IMPETUS OF ITS OWN AND, GROWING WILDER AND WILDER, SOMETIMES LAST SEVERAL DAYS..."
of ECONOMICS, 1958
TODAY'S TEENAGERS ARE ONLY INTERESTED IN ONE THING: THE BEAT."

"I FIRMLY BELIEVE THAT PEOPLE CAN, AND DO, HAVE REVELATORY EXPERIENCES ON THE DANCE FLOOR."
COLIN ANGUS, THE SHAMEN

england

driver

ERVE OVERKILL

THE BRITISH PRESS PACK

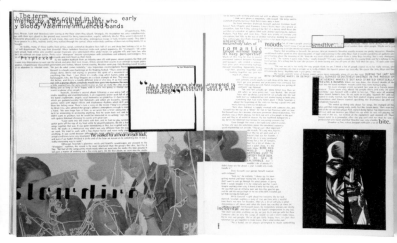

slowdive

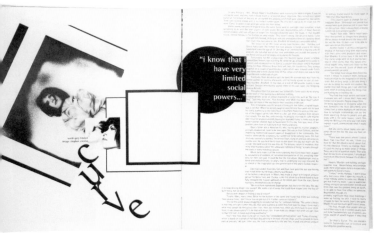

"i know that i have very limited social powers..."

ve

IN LONDON, EVERY OTHER TAXI driver seems

where

?

Stereo stereo hi-fi

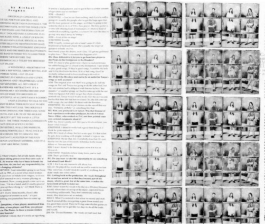

GIVE BARBIE A GUN

WHY ARE THERE NO GUNS FOR BARBIE?
VIOLENCE AGAINST WOMEN IS ON THE RISE
BUT NO ONE HAS ANY IDEA HOW TO STOP IT
I THINK WE COULD HEAR A LOT OF THIS SHIT
OFF AT THE PASS IF WE WOULD JUST
GIVE BARBIE A GUN
I WAS WATCHING TELEVISION RECENTLY AND SOME
MARKETING CLOWN HAS COME UP WITH
ANOTHER BRILLIANT BARBIE CONCEPT;
WHEN YOU ADD WATER OR A MAGNET OR SOMETHING
TO BARBIE'S BOSOM IT MAGICALLY BECOMES
COVERED WITH HEARTS
I WON'T GET INTO THE ZILLIONS OF OCCASIONS
YOUR AVERAGE BARBIE-OWNING YOUNG WOMAN WILL
HAVE THE OPPORTUNITY TO ACTUALLY WEAR A
SWIMSUIT IN HER REAL LIFE, I JUST WANT TO SAY
I THINK IT'S SICK AND PERVERSE THAT BARBIE
BECOMES ALL HEARTS AND SMILES AND FLOWERS
WHEN YOU FUCK WITH HER CLOTHES
WITH A RUST LIKE THAT WHAT BARBIE SHOULD
REALLY BE DOING IS PACKING A PIECE
WHERE'S POLICEWOMAN BARBIE?
WHERE'S COMBAT BARBIE AND
SHARPSHOOTIN' COWGIRL BARBIE?
I WANT TO SEE CATBURGLAR BARBIE AND
DOMINATRIX BARBIE, TRANSFORMER SWAT TEAM
BARBIE
WHOSE ARMS TURN INTO M-16'S AND BREASTS TURN
INTO GRENADES
WHERE'S NAVY ADMIRAL BARBIE WITH HER PINK
TORPEDOES? WHERE'S REVENGE OF THE BOSNIAN
WOMEN'S BARBIE WHO MOWS AROUND THE PLAY-
GROUND
AFTER A BARBIE RIPPING THE BALLS OFF
ALL THE GI JOES?
YOU'LL BE GLAD YOU DID
GIVE BARBIE A GUN
THIS MAY LOOK LIKE AN ORDINARY IMPRACTICAL
UNCOMFORTABLE HIGH-HEELED PUMP TO YOU BUT
IT'S
ACTUALLY A MINI ASSAULT RIFLE
AND TEACH HER TO USE IT
GIVE BARBIE A GUN
AND THEN ASK HER WHY, BLAME IT ALL ON
MALE BASHING BARBIE
GIVE GIVE GIVE
HER
GUN GUN GUN
AND SHE'LL HAVE
FUN FUN FUN
UNTIL HER BARBY TAKES HER UZI AWAY
MAKE IT NOT ENOUGH
GIVE BARBIE A GUN

special privileges. no

Th. Labels within

KILL

"Dumb is great. We love dumb," .... "If you're a REAL ROCK PURIST, as we are, you can't get it dumb enough. When you need that rock fix, you're looking for the dumbest rock you can find, MOTORHEAD or MISFITS or DEVO, or something that's really fucking dumb as shit that makes you feel really intelligent. Rock can't be wrong enough. The lower, the better. That's why bands like the STOOGES and MC5 who went nowhere in their time are being considered legends. There was no demand for it at the time, but now everybody realizes that was a high point for DUMB ROCK."

YOU AM I

finger satellit.

cynthia p caster

COPROLALIA

new 5 track ep out now

rooArt

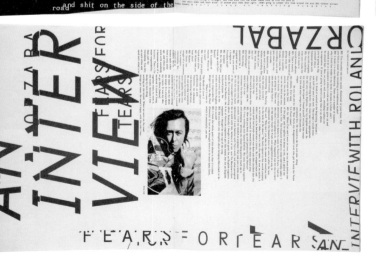

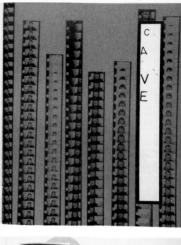

NICK

CAVE

John Huba

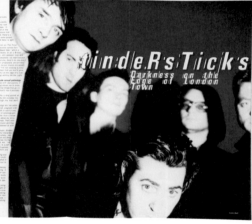

iinde.RsTick's
Darkness on the Edge of London Town

by Michael Bracewell

for those about to rock,
we will eat you.

cradle of thorns

the debutane triffid x.

subsori be rongun

310.452.6222

THIRTY OUGHT SIX

STAR PIMP

THE GTS

RODAN

UNDERWORLD

A
K
A
R
A
O
K
E
R
A
V
E
-
U
P
W
I
T
H
T
H
E
M
U
F
F
S

by Adam Nagel
photos by Michael Miller

PHOTOGRAPHY BY LINDSAY BRICE

DFFFAT

BULLETS ARE THE WINDOW OF THE SOUL (IF YOU LOOK AT SOMEBODY THE WRONG WAY). ACRES OF DEFEAT–TREATISE ON LOS ANGELES. TRICT OR TREAT–CHAOS OR FORGETFULNESS— COMPASSION OR LUST. THIS IS OUR SIDE OF THE BORDER; OUR OWN DISGUST. MEXICO-ENGLISH. COMPUTERIZE LANGUAGE INTO SOUNDSPEAK, CENTURY, CITY, PLAINTIFF. FIRE ON ME AT A STOPLIGHT. OR HIDE IN A WALLED CITY AND WATCH US TURN AGAINST US. BETWEEN THE PIKNSAVE ON LINCOLN AND THE SALVATIONARMY ON 11TH AND OLYMPIC THAT'S

SHONEN KNIFE

Revival of the ROCK POSTER
LA ARTISTS
BY NANCY DWORSKY

SHONEN KNIFE
MONDAY - FEBRUARY 8
1ST SHOW SOLD OUT / 2ND SHOW 10.30
ROXY ALL AGES

i Dig redd Kross
BY Thurston Moore

THE CHURCH

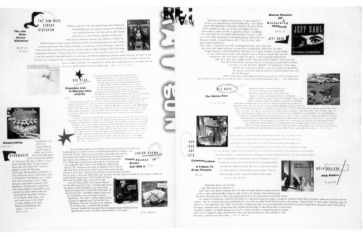

CAR WASH

Fluid in the LUNGS OF TAD

読ませて、感じさせるための革命行為
時代の空気を誌面に落とし込むということ

「僕のレイアウトが、書かれた記事に敬意を払わないものだと人々は言うけれど、本当はまったく逆だと思うんだ。例えば音楽についてであれば、その音楽にどっぷり浸かりながら届いた記事を読んでいると、生まれてくる感情というものがある。僕はそれにできるだけ正直に感応し、デザインの力でいかに読み手をその環境に引き込むかを意識して作っている。写真やイラストレーション、それからタイポグラフィーを使って、ページに感情を注入するんだ」

そう語るのは、90年代を代表する音楽雑誌界の寵児『RAYGUN』の初期アートディレクターであったデヴィッド・カーソンだ。立ち上げから関わった『RAYGUN』における彼の存在は、細分化されたアメリカの雑誌編集部には珍しく、写真編集、誌面デザイン、編集方針に至るまで、本当に統括的なものだった。

「『RAYGUN』で与えられていた自由は、実にユニークなものだったと思う。ページを作り込んで、誰の許可を仰ぐこともなく、そのまま印刷所に送ればよかった。カバーのロゴだって毎回違ったし、とにかくその時代の音楽の持つ空気を、よりリアルに伝える雑誌にしたかったんだ。ある人は僕が公衆を相手に大掛かりな実験をしてるって言ってたね」

始まりは『Beach Culture』

そもそも『RAYGUN』発行人の目に留まったのは、デヴィッドが手掛けた『Beach Culture』という伝説のコースタルライフ誌だった。南カリフォルニアにあるサーフ専門誌の裏倉庫で、編集者とほぼ2人で作り上げた雑誌で、1989年から3年間で6冊のみの発行だが、デヴィッドは今でも『RAYGUN』以上の完成度を自負している。

「予算がない中で絞り出すように発行していた『Beach Culture』を、僕は毎回 "最終号" というつもりで取り組んだんだ。この雑誌の立ち上げの噂を聞き、ニューヨークから、1年間離れていたカリフォルニアへ戻ってきた。昼も夜も関係なく、食べることも忘れてレイアウトに没頭したものだよ。貧乏だったけど、心から好きなことをやっているという充足感はすごくあった。自分の力を発揮し切れる環境が与えられるということは、本当に大切なことなんだと知ったよ」

サーフィンからデザインへのシフトチェンジ

サーフ、スケートボード、音楽、そしてコースタルライフを誌面につめ込んだ『Beach Culture』は、西海岸でサーフィンに没頭して育ったカーソンの全力投球によって実ったものだった。10代の頃からプロサーファーとして大会に出て、寝ても覚めても海一色だった彼は、26歳になったある日、生まれて初めてグラフィックデザインという分野を知ったという。

「それまでそんな仕事があること自体知らなかった。過去20年

間のサーフ雑誌はどれもキャプションを暗唱できるほど喰い入るように眺めてきたけれど、それはタイポグラフィーに興味があるという種類のものではなかったんだ。友人の紹介で始めた雑誌のインターンが、この世界の入口になった。それを知ってからというもの、これまでサーフィンに注ぎ込んできたエネルギーの全てがグラフィックデザインに移行したんだ。大学で社会学を専攻していたから、商品パッケージとしてのデザインより、実社会で起こっていることや生まれてくる音楽をデザインで解釈する方が、僕にとっては面白かったんだね。気づいたら雑誌の世界にいて、それがごく自然なことのような気がしたんだ」

きっかけになったインターンも雑誌自体がなくなり、デヴィッドは数年間サンディエゴの高校で社会学を教えることになった。その間にも彼はスイスで行われたデザインワークショップなどに参加している。そのうちに『Transworld Skateboard』誌からアートディレクションの仕事が入り、教員を辞めて、1983年からの4年間はデザインに没頭。その後、あえてスケートやスノーボードの世界から自分を切り離すべく、ニューヨークの音楽雑誌『Musician』のオファーを受けて東へ移住。そして『Beach Culture』の誕生とともに、再び西海岸へ戻ってくることになる。

『RAYGUN』とデヴィッド・ボウイの首

『RAYGUN』は90年代というグランジミュージックを生み出した時代を駆け抜けた。創刊から4年にわたり、その顔とも言える表紙と誌面をデザインしてきたデヴィッドにとって、そこを離れる原因となったのは、30号目のデヴィッド・ボウイのカバーだったという。

「写真が編集部に届けられ、カメラを見据えたデヴィッド・ボウイの写真がほとんどの中に、見た瞬間『これがカバーだ！』と確信した1枚があったんだ。それは彼の首のショットだった。これまで顔半分などはやってきたけれど、そんなものを吹き飛ばしてしまうような強さを感じたよ。ところが彼の大ファンでもあった発行人たちが、この号に限って表紙に待ったをかけたんだ。『それじゃ誰だかわからない』って。結局最後まで譲らずにカバーデザインを拒む中、彼らは普通にカメラを覗き込むボウイの写真を表紙に使った。僕はそれで興味をすっかりなくしてしまったし、発行人側も次号のレイアウトを送ってこなかった。確かにこの一件がなければまだ続けていたかもしれないけれど、それだけこの写真には強いこだわりを持っていたんだ。今でもあれがカバーになっていたらと考えてしまうよ」

そう口惜しそうに笑みを浮かべた。結局目次ページで使われた首の写真は、デヴィッドの書籍『End of Print』にも登場している。『Beach Culture』と同じ卓上で作られた1号目、借りてきたコンピューターに入っていた5つのフォントだけで誌面を作った2号目（「そういうチャレンジを自分に課すのが好きなんだ」とカーソン……。）様々なパーソナルな歴史をも反映してきた。その号のために買い集めた音楽に聴き入り、部屋全体をぐちゃぐちゃにしながら作り上げてきた『RAYGUN』中心の生活。そこから離れて広告仕事にシフトすることで、また新たなリズムが生まれた。冬場は波を求めてカリブ海に面する別宅に飛ぶなど、再びサーフィンを楽しむ時間ができたという。「10代の"これしかなかった"というサーフィンの時代から、ぐるりと一周した感じだね」と語る口調も穏やかだ。

"印刷の終焉（End of Print）"の、そのまた先

現在スイス・チューリッヒにも仕事の拠点を置き、映像や広告、エディトリアルデザインを手掛けているデヴィッドだが、今回はサウスキャロライナのフォリー・ビーチにある自宅兼アトリエを訪れた。東海岸特有の蒸し暑さがピークに達した6月初旬、屋外デッキには格子を通して、オフセットプリントを拡大したときのような円状の光が差し込んでいた。オーストリアの建築学生を招いて作ったというデッキと光の関係は、どことなく彼自身のデザイン美学に通じるところがある。「似ているのは、後からの影響を考えて作るという部分かな。明らかに目に見えるものだけじゃなく、何かを内包しているデザインなんだ」。木々に囲まれたその場所で、手紙を読んだり朝食を楽しんだりするという。庭にはワークショップで出かけた土地で目に留まったものがひっそりと置かれている。パナマの看板職人に作らせた講演告知の手描き看板や、ブラジルの道端でまさに取り払われようとしていた幾重にも糊付けされた紙ポスターの破片など、行く先々で身の回りの風景をスキャンしている様子が目に浮かぶ。『RAYGUN』を見たネビル・ブロディに『行き着くところまで行き着いた、これは印刷の終焉（End of Print）そのものだ』と言わせ、デビット・バーン（元トーキングヘッズ）には『印刷は解放された。従来のニュースだけを伝える義務から、解き放たれたのだ』と言わしめた独自のデザイン。音楽雑誌という広く大衆の手に渡るメディアでのデザイン革命は、無類の賞賛の声があがる一方で、既存の権威には畏怖心を与え、ある美術学校ではあまりのラディカルさにご法度になったという。「それがたとえ嫌悪感であったとしても、『RAYGUN』で僕のやろうとしたことが、それだけ中軸を打ったということだよね」とデヴィッドは静かに笑う。

David Carson

Born 1956 in Texas. Received a BFA in sociology from San Diego State University. Being also a professional surfer from his college days, David made Southern California the base for his graphic design work, attracting attention for his radical editorial design for *Beach Culture* and *RAYGUN*. He later moved his bases to New York and South Carolina and in addition to graphic design expanded his activities to incude art direction, film direction and lecturing. He is currently based in Zurich and Portland. His accolades run the gamut of professional worlds and exceed 170 to date. He is the author of *The End of Print* among others.

デヴィッド・カーソン

1956年アメリカ、テキサス州生まれ。NYを経てサンディエゴ州立大学にて社会学学位を取得。学生時代からプロサーファーでもあったことから、その後南カリフォルニアをベースにグラフィックデザインを手掛け、『Beach Culture』や『RAYGUN』などの斬新なエディトリアルデザインで注目される。その後NYとサウスキャロライナにベースを移し、グラフィックデザインはもとより、アートディレクター、映像監督、講師として活躍。現在はチューリヒ、ポートランドを拠点にしている。各界からの受賞も多く、総数はこれまでに170を超えるという。著書に『The End of Print』など。

松本弦人

GENTO MATSUMOTO

(RITS, B)

Piles of sketchbooks overflowing with ideas, made real by the craftsmanship of the designer

Gento Matsumoto is somewhat of a maverick among the designers featured here. Although best known for his video games and prodigiously imaginative artworks such as those using bin liners, what caught my particular attention was his background in magazine design. Following designer jobs for *Number* and *Marie Claire*, in 1991 he launched *RITS*, a new computer-aided fashion magazine. Fifteen years later, in the magazine *B* published to mark the 30th anniversary of clothing retailers BEAMS, once again Matsumoto is deploying his outstanding armory of design skills. At first glance the layout of *B* appears disorderly, but as always the designer's excellent grounding in basic design know-how and ability to make that extra imaginative leap beyond the conventional shine through.

— When I imagine you as a magazine revolutionary, the first thing that comes to mind is *RITS*, which was awesome. One of the best magazines ever, in my opinion.
"The design for *RITS* really revealed the computer in the raw, I think. Using the computer became a bit of an obsession, and the result was this feeling of having really wrung all the juice out of it. Until then nobody had used a computer to produce a magazine, and the layouts for *RITS* were submitted to the printer not as data, but printed out first on film. The mechanicals for the opening page were done using a laser writer and enlarged for printing, so the text tended to be a bit fuzzy. Well, this was back in the '90s, after all. The editor Fumihiro Hayashi and I had some massive rows along the way, me being angrily accused of just doing whatever I felt like. But when I met him five or six years later, he told me that now he actually quite likes the way the magazine worked out.
During my time at Propeller Art Works, before *RITS* that

is, the need for design to be neat and tidy was constantly drummed into us, so perhaps I was rebelling against that. At Propeller, as you can imagine I did my best to learn the tone of my mentor there, Naomi Enami. That three-and-a-half years was the most concentrated period of study in my career, so it still provides the foundation of what I do today, but when I left to work for myself I was keen to try my luck with something different."

The appearance of *B*, spiritual heir of *RITS*

— For 15 years until *B*, you were out of magazines altogether, weren't you? When I saw *B*, I perceived something of the same spirit as *RITS*. Then when I saw the name Gento Matsumoto in the credits, I thought, aha, now I know why.
"When I was introduced for the first time at a BEAMS meeting, I told them it was 15 years since I'd had anything to do with either fashion or magazines, so if they didn't mind I'd be treating the experience a bit like rehab (laughs). Actually when I was working on *B* I didn't have a single copy of *RITS* on hand. But now that you mention it, there are similarities. It's as if the culture and fashion of *RITS* have melded into the new magazine.
In both games and magazines, my main interest has always been how something works as a medium. *B* had its beginnings in the BEAMS president's powerful urge to produce a magazine to mark their 30th anniversary. These days it seems all the villains want a slice of the media action (laughs). But seriously, that's actually a really good thing in my view, and media motivated by that sort of personal ambition tend to fare the best. It's like in surfing: if an interesting wave comes along you ride it, even at the risk of wiping out."

— When you put together a magazine as art director, do you have an image in mind beforehand of how you want to do it?

"Quite often, yes. For *B* I attempted to suggest a different sort of medium by printing what I guess you'd call fashion photographs on grainy paper, in a B5 format like that used for weeklies. I knew right from the start that's what I wanted to do. It had to be small, and easy enough to pick up in Harajuku and throw away by the time you reached Sugamo while going round the Yamanote Line. So it was OK for the design to look cool, but no point being too stylish (laughs). It was to be like the photo spreads of a youth magazine, while maintaining a certain minimum BEAMS tone. BEAMS was very much against using a B5 format, but I just had this totally groundless conviction that it would work. It required a fair bit of negotiation with the editor Nakajima-san. At that stage, on one hand I felt confident we could create something totally new, and on the other, I was just bluffing my way through.

The other amazing thing was setting up an editorial department right in the BEAMS pressroom. You couldn't ask for a better environment. The BEAMS staff were right there to give their gut reactions, and the designers, editors and writers all passed in and out of there. I'd always imagined myself to be especially scrupulous about the location and environment when making things, but that editor was way better at it than me. It struck me as a great way to create a sense of up-to-the-minute relevancy."

— So that's the environment you were working in. That sense of immediacy does come through in the magazine.

Still happiest when drawing

— Where do you get your actual page design ideas from?

"(Pulling out a huge pile of notebooks) By drawing in these sketchbooks, my secret notebooks I guess you'd call them. I suppose I sort of think with my hands. My father's a painter, and had me doing oil paintings from age five. So when I'm in a work meeting I can sketch something on the spot, which of course speeds up the discussion. I'm not very good at explaining things in words. I employ this draw and show approach – ideal for me personally – for ads, Websites, games. By the time I've filled a notebook, I've usually worked out the finished look. I then use the sketches as the basis for the photo shoot for example, and even if I'm not able to be present for the shoot, it's interesting to see the essence of what I've drawn emerging. I churn out sketches at a terrific rate; when I'm drawing is when I'm happiest."

— Wow, this is amazing! It's the first time I've seen someone in my line of work do this. You're more artist than designer.

"Although I'd rather not describe myself as such, I admit if you ask me what I do, I'm never sure whether to say drawing or making. Yet I am more interested in the overall texture and sense of media than the balance of the design. I hardly ever see magazines or movies or such, so I really don't have many inputs. You Fujimoto-san arm yourself perfectly with templates and editorial design schemes and the like; I on the other hand haven't assembled much of that, so rather than constructing a clearly-defined format, I just throw it all together based on factors like how the photos will work, and my ideas. And in terms of design, as long as the elements are right, it'll work out somehow. That's my philosophy. For *B*, I started with the basic elements of choosing a special font just for that one issue, and making sure the photos had a consistent look. A bit ad hoc I guess, but there you have it."

The craftsmanship to make ideas reality

— Apart from your drawing, do you take photos or anything like that?

"I do indeed take photos. But I detest my own pictures. They're actually quite good, but that's precisely what I dislike about them. They look like exactly the sort of pictures a designer would take (laughs). I guess I have a few I can use as photos for design work. I just take them as I go along, in the same way that I do rough sketches, using the camera to capture things I can't work out how to sketch. It's only being interviewed like this I realize: I'm not a typical magazine designer, am I?"

— But the way that very individuality is reflected in the magazines is what makes your work so great. You have a style, but at the same time, these sudden left-field flashes of inspiration.

"I do enjoy coming up with out of this world stuff. But ideas must be interesting, otherwise they're not ideas. And the other thing you need is the technical skills to convert those ideas into tangible form. Even a slight slip in the printing can render a brilliant idea worthless. In the end it is the craftsmanship drummed into us, and the things we've studied, that sustain our work.

I admit I had Gento Matsumoto down as a somewhat of a rebel. But he preps meticulously for his art direction work, and that seriousness is channeled to stunning effect into his design. Seeing that mountain of sketches, I felt I'd gained a privileged glimpse into the secret behind the explosive imaginative power of this one-of-a-kind designer.

TAKEO KIKUCHI
Printemps Ete Collection

World Co.,Ltd. TK Division
World Nishiazabu Bldg., 4-3-5 Nishiazabu,
Minato-ku Tokyo Phone 03.3407.1371

HIROYUKI NAKANO

ALAIN MIKLI

FABRICE BER'GER-REMOND

TONY MENEGUZZO

PAUL SMITH FRIENDS
CRAIG RICHARDS

DIRECTOR'S GALLERY
KAZUHIRO KOBAYASHI

Obscure Desire

SaLSa

058

TROPIC

STEVEN MEISEL INTERVIEW

90年代に要求されるのは、"超時的な力"である。

私は博物館に、人間の残像には出ない隠された美を出そうと思っている。

美を共規化する時代の寵児

Crawl out now, King Snake!

06

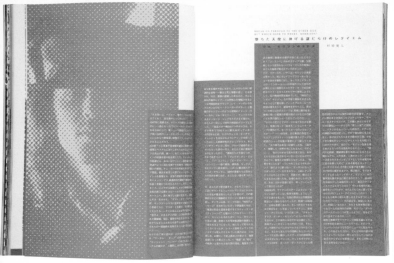

The Superior RITZ
SPRING/SUMMER 1991 No.1

NEXT
The Superior RITZ
AUTUMN 1991 No.

ASPIRIN AGE

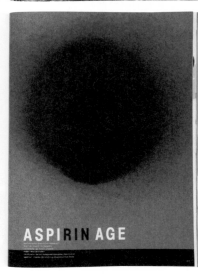

STEVEN KLEIN

がらくたの街、ニューヨークを舞台にした「パラダイス」。
写真：神保麻子　文：所内弘之

GO TO NEW WORK

STAY FREE

SUNDAY MORNING

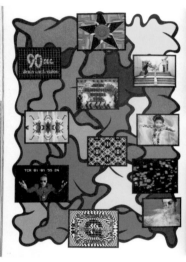

See Gee GeN

NO SENSE = NO MONEY?

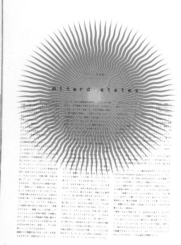

DRUG CHOCOLATE

black and blood

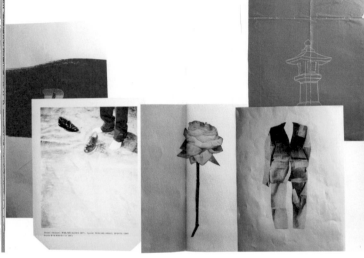

white and blood

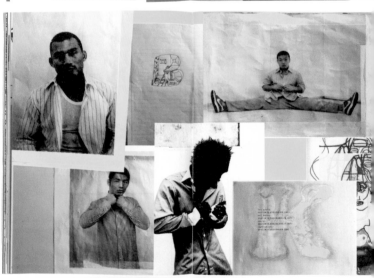

チクジョウセヨ！

Shi-RO-SOUL

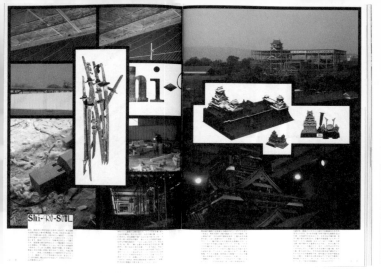

Shi-RO-SOUL

photo yasumura takashi
HOUSE IN A SUBURB OF TOKYO
SILENT AND POLITE SYSTEM
A CONTINUOUS SOUND OF TREES
THEY LIVE

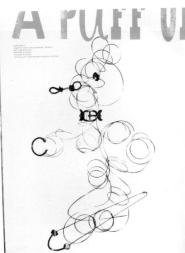

A PUFF OF SPRING

ChATTY GiRLhood

MULTIPLE APPLE

photo WATARU (eigh: peace)
styling takeda :oihio (mild)
model: Marcelina, Eva P, Aanna, Gabriera O,Lena v, Machida
hair and make up: kema katsuya
hair : ABU
make up: YUKI

FRUiTS OF ANALYSiS

06

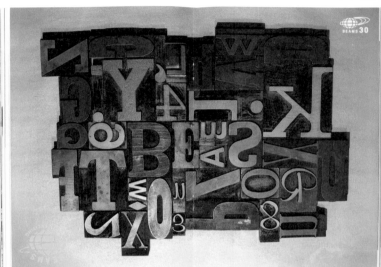

apple

1976年

ガレージから生まれたパーソナルコンピュータの登場が後の世界を大きく変えた。

LOVE STORIES

ガラスの仮面

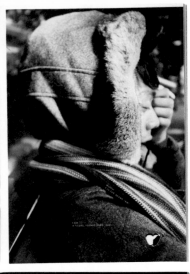

A GIFT

ギフトとその障壁

文：台場伸弘

Gift for the Day

photo P.M.Ken ... styling sanbongi sumi

Gift for the Day

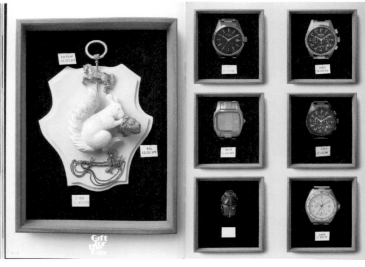

Gift for the Day

merry Xmas

happy
Xmas
solution
company.

BEAMS 30TH

to fill your
christmas eve
with happiness.

to fill your mail artifat from everyone.

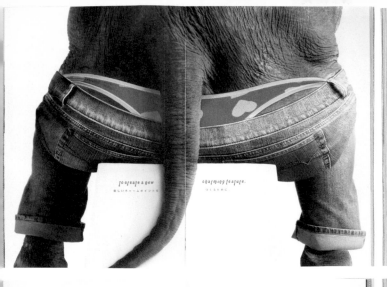

to create a new   charming feature.
新しいチャームポイントを   つくるために。

to say good-bye   to your inconspicuous self.
目立たない自分に   さよならするために。

Suits You Best!
やんちゃなスーツ

Suits You Best!

忌野清志郎になりそこねた男。

これまたひどく陽気な、いや殺伐とした叫び声が聞こえてきた! 暴動だ!!

HArD MAN F: DEAD (Hard Version)

T.SHiRTs & T.rumps

Tシャツとトランプ。

DReSs Me HAPPY

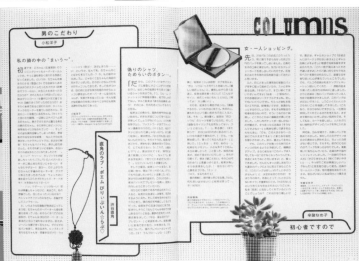

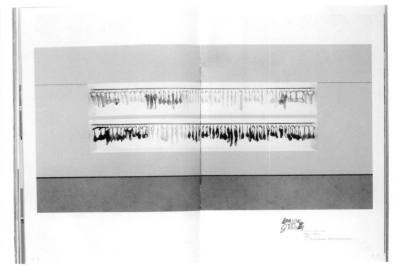

膨大な量のスケッチブックからアイデアが溢れ出し
デザインにおける職人性がその実現を支えている

　今回のデザイナーの中では異端の人だ。ゲームデザインやゴミ袋など、超人的なアイデアを持つ作品で知られているが、意外にも雑誌デザイン出身ということで注目していた。『ナンバー』や『マリ・クレール』のデザイナーを経て、91年にコンピューターを使った新しいファッション誌『RITS』を立ち上げる。その15年後に手掛けたBEAMSの30周年記念誌『B』でも、際立ったデザイン力を発揮。一見無秩序なレイアウトだが、確かな知識とそれを超越した発想を感じずにはいられないのだ。

——雑誌の革命児として松本さんを捉えたときに、まず思い起こすのが『RITS』のすごさ。ボクは最大の評価をしています。

　「このデザインはコンピューターの生身の部分がそのまま出てますね。相当はまっていたので、その汁が出まくっちゃった感じ。それまでは雑誌をコンピューターで作る人なんていなくて、データではなく、一度フィルム出力したものを入稿していたんです。巻頭はレーザーライターで描き出した版下を拡大プリントしているので、文字がボソボソしてしまったり。90年代だからしょうがないですよね。編集長の林文浩さんとは大喧嘩しながら進めました。好き勝手やりやがって、みたいな感じで怒られて。でも5〜6年後にお会いしたときには『今になって、実は結構気に入っている』と言っていただいた。

　『RITS』以前のプロペラアートワークス時代は、美しく整然と

したデザインを叩き込まれていたので、その反動かもしれませんね。プロペラでは師の江並直美さんのトーンを一生懸命学ぶじゃないですか。その3年半は本当に一番の勉強期間だったから、今も自分の基礎として支えになっていますが、独立したときに違う部分で勝負したいという思いがありました」

『RITS』スピリットを受け継ぐ『B』の登場

——15年後の『B』まで、雑誌から離れてますよね。『B』を見たとき『RITS』と同じ魂みたいなものを感じたんです。で、クレジットを見たら松本弦人と書いてあって、やっぱりなって。

　「最初にBEAMSのミーティングで紹介されたとき、ファッションも雑誌も15年ぶりなので、リハビリみたいな感じでやるのでよろしくお願いしますって挨拶しました(笑)。実は『B』を進めているときには『RITS』は一冊も手元になかったんです。でも言われてみると似てますね。『RITS』のカルチャーとファッションが融合した感じとか。

　ずっとそうなんですが、ゲームにしろ雑誌にしろ、僕が興味あるのはメディアとしての在り方なんです。『B』はBEAMSの30周年を記念して雑誌を作りたいという、社長の強い希望からスタートしてます。今どき悪者はメディアを持ちたがるじゃないですか(笑)。いや、それはすごいよいことだなと思っていて、そんな個人的な欲望を動機としたメディアは強いんです。サーフィ

ンで言えば面白い波がきて、これは失敗してでも乗っておくでしょみたいな感覚」

——アートディレクターという立場で1冊を作る際に、こういう風にしようってイメージを事前に頭の中で決めるんですか？

「それは結構ありますね。『B』は週刊誌風のB5判でざらっとした紙質に、いわゆるファッション写真を刷ることで違うメディア感を出そうとしたんです。それはもう最初からイメージしていて。小さくて、原宿で手に入れて山手線の巣鴨でもう捨てちゃうような手軽さ。だからデザインはカッコよくてもいいんだけど、お洒落は禁止（笑）。ヤングマガジンのグラビアページみたいな感じで、最低限のBEAMSのトーンは守る。絶対にB5判はないってBEAMSにも反対されたけど、根拠のない自信はありました。絶対これって。編集長の中島さんと俺とで、ずいぶん交渉しましたよ。その時点では新しいモノになる自信とハッタリと、両方ですね。

あとすごいのが、BEAMSのプレスルームの中に編集部を作っちゃったんですよ。それはもう最高の環境。BEAMSスタッフから直の反応があって、そこにデザイナーも編集者もライターも通って。自分もモノを作るときの場所や環境には気を遣っているつもりだったけど、そのときの編集長の方が完全に上手でした。今な感じの作り方だなって感心しました」

——そういう環境でやってたんですね。そのライブ感みたいなのが出ています。

絵を描いてるときが、今でも一番楽しい

——具体的なページデザインのアイデアは、どこから生まれてくるのですか？

「（膨大な量のノートを取り出して）ヒミツのノートっていうか、スケッチブックに絵を描くことで、手癖で考えるみたいなところがありますね。親父が絵描きで、5歳のときから油絵描かされてたんです。だから打合せしながらその場で描いたりして、それを見せると話が早いじゃないですか。言葉で説明するのは苦手なので。自分にとって得意な絵を描いて見せるというやり方は、広告でもWEBでもゲームでも同じですね。ノートを1冊描き上げると、だいたいイメージは完成します。それをもとに撮影したり、もし撮影に立ち会えなくても、自分が描いたもののエキスが出てると面白いじゃないですか。ガンガン描いてますよ。描いてるときが一番楽しいですね」

——すごいねこれ！同業者でこうやってる人を初めてみた。デザイナーというよりアーティストに近いね。

「あまりそういう言い方はしたくないんですけれど、やってることと言えば、ずっと描いてるか作ってるかですね。それでいてデザインのバランスより、全体の質感やメディア感に興味がある。雑誌や映画はほとんど見ないので、インプットは相当少ないと思います。藤本さんはテンプレートやエディトリアルデザインの構図みたいなものが完全に武器になっていますよね。自分の場合は、あまりそれをためてこなかったので、確固としたフォーマットを構築していくというよりは、撮影の仕方とかアイデアだけでどんと成立させちゃう。それでデザイン的にはエレメントだけはっきりさせておけば、何とかなっちゃうでしょという考え方。『B』では1冊ごとに特殊なフォントを用意するのと、写真のテイストを統一させるというエレメントをベースに進めたんです。大雑把といえば大雑把ですよね」

アイデアを実現するのに必要な職人性

——絵以外に、写真を撮ったりはしないんですか？

「写真は撮りますよ。だけど自分の写真が大嫌いで。そこそこ上手くて、でもそこが嫌で。デザイナーの写真だなみたいな（笑）。デザインのための写真として使えるものはいくつかあるよなって感じですね。ラフを描くようにネチネチ撮ってみて、ラフだと思いつけないことを写真で掴み取るイメージかな。こうやって藤本さんにインタビューされると、確かに普通の雑誌デザインの人とは違いますね」

——その個性が誌面に反映されているのがすごいよね。スタイルがあって、でもポコーンと出てきたような閃きのアイデアがある。

「世の中にないものを考えるのは好きですね。でも、アイデアが面白いのは当たり前で、面白くないのはアイデアじゃない。そこでもう1つ必要になるのが、それを形にする技術。印刷のさじ加減一つでも、同じアイデアがどうにでもなってしまう。そこを支えるのは、やっぱり叩き込まれた職人性と勉強した部分なんですよね」

ボクは彼に無頼派なイメージを持っていた。だけど、そのアートディレクションにはきちんとした準備があり、その生真面目さはデザインに生かされている。圧倒的な量のスケッチを前にして、アイデアにおける瞬発力の秘訣に触れた気がした。

Gento Matsumoto
Born 1961 in Tokyo. Graduated from the Kuwasawa Institute of Design. Established Sarubrunei Co., Ltd. in 1990 where he art directs advertising, books, filmic and digital media projects. Matsumoto's major digital media works include the Pop up Computer floppy disk, the Jungle Park CD-ROM (Digitalogue), and the Dobutsu Bancho series for Nintendo Cube game machines. He is the author of *Matsumoto Gento: Shigoto to sono shuhen* (Gento Matsumoto: Work and its fringes). Among the many honors he has received are the New York Disk of the Year Grand Prix, the Yomiuri Shimbun Award, the 1995 Tokyo ADC Award, the Best Visual Designer for 1996 at the AMD Awards, and the 2002 Tokyo TDC Award.

松本弦人
1961年東京生まれ。桑沢デザイン研究所卒。1990年株式会社サルブルネイ設立。広告、書籍、映像、デジタルメディアのアートディレクションを手掛ける。主なデジタルメディア作品に、フロッピーディスク『Pop up Computer』、CD-ROM『ジャングルパーク』（デジタローグ）、ゲームソフト『動物番長』（Nintendoキューブ）、著書に『松本弦人仕事とその周辺』（六耀社）がある。NEW YORK DISK OF THE YEAR グランプリ、読売新聞社賞、1995年ADC賞、AMD Award '96 Best Visual Designer、2002年 Tokyo TDC 賞など受賞多数。

羽良多平吉

heiQuiti HARATA

(HEAVEN, ガロ)

GARO

Bringing the concept of editorial to design.
We have to expand it to that extent.

I associate the name of the graphic designer, heiQuiti HARATA, with the words "legendary designer". The magazine *HEAVEN*, which was first issued in 1980, only had nine editions and what's more was one of those erotic magazines you buy from vending machines. Even so, I often hear it being mentioned by young editorial designers as their favorite magazine and even now they're being traded on the internet at high prices. That's the stuff of legend. My personal opinion is that the unique use of color is impressive and that they had a beauty that transcended the times in the design style of the typography. Firstly, I'm going to ask him how he became associated with *HEAVEN*.

The magnetic force of Kosakusha

— What's the story behind you firstly becoming an editorial designer and then becoming involved with *HEAVEN*?"
"Because I had only studied crafts at university, I had to learn all the complex language of graphics from the technical people on the job. In the process, I used to hang out with the editors and found myself in a totally unexpected place.
With *HEAVEN* too, an acquaintance introduced me to the editor-in-chief the magazine *Yu*, which was published by Kosakusha and I went to meet him. When I

arrived at Kosakusha, suddenly all the staff started filing down from the second floor and sitting down around me. That's the first time something like that had ever happened to me and it really took me aback. I found out later that as it was a workshop, that sort of thing happened all the time. And, when Seigow Matsuoka who was the editor-in-chief at the time came sauntering down the stairs carrying a manuscript was the first time I laid eyes on him. After that during the next one to two years, I was a frequent visitor to Kosakusha."

— In those days, there was a movement at Kosakusha with *Yu* at the core. There's a feeling that something fresh was created from that. Various people were attracted there ...
"One time we recruited Junnichiro Sanai (Dan Takasugi), Harumi Yamazaki and Shinnosuke Misawa at the magazine. It was at Kosakusha that I also met Hiroshi Aramata and Kohei Sugiura. I'm not sure whether it was fresh or not, but I was pulled in by the mysterious magnetic force of *Yu* and Kosakusha. I distinctly remember it, standing in the bookstore as a high-school student and reading the first issue of *Yu* and *Hanashi no Tokushu*. And then when I heard Matsuoka-san's voice on the phone to me late at night asking me if I wanted to join the very Kosakusha I had visited the previous day, I was there."

— It did have some kind of mysterious attraction, didn't it?

"Now it's totally different but at the time we first learned the true meaning of editorial engineering or we worked with an understanding of it – including design of course and editorial. You could call it a workshop. While my ideas on that kind of editorial design were developing, *HEAVEN* started up at Gunyusha, but my job at Kosakusha was what I would have to call "effect". Something like a recording studio guy who produces sound effects. When I think about it now, the elements that were missing at Kosakusha at the time were fashionableness and the music we were listening to. Surely Matsuoka-san must have known that those elements were indispensable to editorial. In that respect, I don't know how much of that I was able to shoulder, but there were people who clearly recognized my contribution."

— It was indeed very strong in the academic and ethnic arena, but didn't really give a stylish impression.

His style of design

— I'm inspired by designers with a style, like you. Where did that style come from?"

"I think you understand because you have experienced the era of mechanical art, but it started from having a blank mechanical board in front of me and using a Rapidograph pen, first drawing the trim and registration lines. It's a way of designing that's almost unthinkable nowadays. To sum it up, design work was sort of like putting together a collage. In the sense that we had to fit certain contents into one space, it was perhaps like editing. And the problem was how to fit it into the space. If a certain person has his or her own way of achieving that, maybe you could call that a style? If that's what it is, now I have gone back to the design style of monochrome times, with *HEAVEN* as my turning point. I feel as if I am riding on some kind of natural providence that is inside me."

— Your design style wasn't initially the *HEAVEN* design style?

"No, it wasn't. So, when I now look at my design then, it feels close and far away. My taste has completely changed. Now I am designing with a lot more white space. That said, I was originally of the Swiss graphics vein. In my high school days, I used to go to exhibitions and buy catalogues. But I didn't like the design of the catalogues. So I placed white or black paper on the cover and did some lettering in poster colors. The basic design concept at that time was Swiss graphics. So that

was considerably different from my design in the days of *HEAVEN*."

— So you originally you had a Swiss graphic monochrome foundation, with a period of polychrome intermediate colors, but now have you returned to white. How did such a drastic change occur?"

"It's only been a few years since the design industry became digitalized. The world has been taken over by digital technology, and it's only relatively recently that the fuss has calmed down. In other words, the roots for digitalized fonts lie in typography and so Swiss graphics also naturally enter as an element. I suppose you could say that's an opportunity for me. Digitalization has meant a natural return to design in the days before *HEAVEN* ..."

The driving force of doing things by hand

— We've changed to computer-produced graphics, but how have things changed?"

"It has changed. Everything had to change including the finished product. It's not just about expanding possibilities in a good direction but also change in the two vectors of reality and ideals. Particularly now, there's a strong movement back towards the good points of the handmade. When I worked on *HEAVEN*, it was half digital and half analog. That was the ideal format for me. I felt extremely driven. There is not such a sense of satisfaction using only computers.

— It's a question I should have asked at the beginning, but do you actually like producing magazines? (laughs)

"There's nothing more interesting. What am I supposed to say to that question? You and I both have committed ourselves fully to the concept of editorial. The idea of bringing the concept of editorial to design is called editorial design, I think. We have to expand it to that extent. If we try to define what a designer is, information can be broadly classified into text and images. How we combine those two things: add, subtract, multiply, divide, or differentiate and integrate. The interesting part of how you're going to drive that only exists in editorial design."

I finished the interview with the feeling that heiQuiti HARATA was a person of great talent. He has an extraordinary talent for color ideas and construction. He's not too bothered by current trends but rather what he personally likes. Does that sound misleading? I feel from his character and design the existence of images that are visible only to him and of a special world that he has been protecting all along.

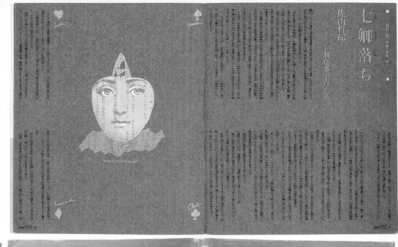

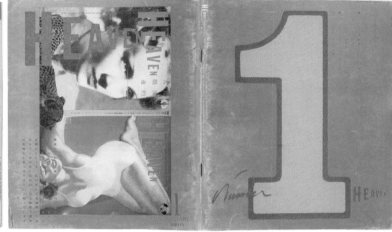

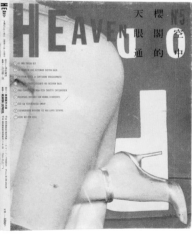

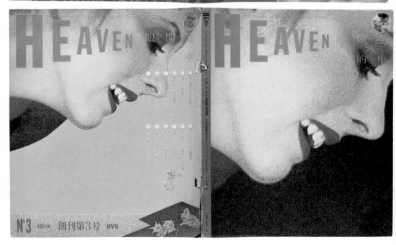

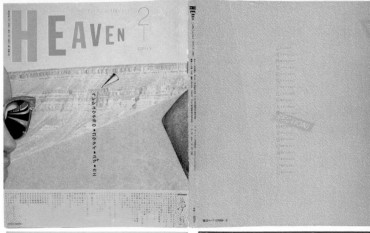

編集という概念をデザインに持ち込む
そこまで広げないと面白くないんじゃないかな

　羽良多平吉さんの名前を聞くと、"伝説のデザイナー"という言葉を連想する。1980年創刊の雑誌『HEAVEN』は9冊しか出されていない。しかも自販機系のエロ雑誌ときている。それにも関わらず、若いエディトリアルデザイナーの好きな雑誌としてしばしばその名を耳にするし、今でもネット上では高い値段で取り引きされている。それが伝説たる由縁だ。個人的な感想を言えば、独特の色使いが印象的で、タイポグラフィーのデザインスタイルには時代を超えた美しさがあると思う。まずは彼が『HEAVEN』に携わるようになったきっかけから聞いてみよう。

工作舎が持っていた磁力

──そもそもエディトリアルデザイナーになり、『HEAVEN』に関わるようになったきっかけは何ですか？

　「僕は大学では工芸しかやらなかったから、グラフィックの細かい手法は、100パーセント現場の職人さんから教えてもらったんですね。それを体得しながら編集者と付き合っていたら、とんでもないところに来ちゃったな、という感じ。『HEAVEN』も、知人の紹介で工作舎が出版していた雑誌『遊』の編集長に会いに行ったのがきっかけ。工作舎に行くと、突然、ドドドってスタッフが全員、2階から降りてきて、僕の周りに座りだしたんです。そんな体験は初めてだったので、もうびっくりしちゃって。あとで知らされたのだけど、ワークショップだったため、そういうことは普通のことだったみたいで。で、当時の編集長だった松岡正剛さんが原稿を持ってゆっくりと降りてこられ

て、それが初対面でしたね。それから1〜2年の間、工作舎にはしょっちゅう出入りしてたな」

──あの頃は、工作舎の『遊』を核にしたムーブメントが起きてましたね。何か新鮮なものが、あそこから生まれていたという印象があります。そこにいろいろな人が惹き付けられて集まって……。

　「あるとき、雑誌でスタッフ募集をしたことがあって、佐内順一郎(高杉 弾)君や山崎春美君、美沢真之助君が集まってきたわけです。荒俣 宏さんや、杉浦康平さんとお会いしたのも工作舎でしたね。新鮮かどうかはわからないけど、僕自身『遊』や、工作舎という不思議な磁力を浴びていました。はっきり覚えているんですけど、高校時代に本屋で『遊』や『話の特集』の創刊号を立ち読みしてたんですよ。それで結局、あの工作舎を訪ねたその翌日の深夜通信での松岡さんの、『一緒にやらない?』なんて一言で引きずり込まれちゃった」

──何か不思議な魔力があったんでしょうね。

　「当時は今の状況とはまったく違って、エディトリアル・エンジニアリングとはどういうものなのかということを実感してから、あるいは実感しながら作業する感覚でしたね。デザインはもちろん編集も含めて。いわゆるワークショップです。そんな編集デザインに対する思いがつのるうち、郡雄社で『HEAVEN』が始まったんですけど、工作舎での僕の役割は"効果"、つまりエフェクトだったんじゃないかな。例えるなら効果音を出すスタジオマ

ンみたいなもの。今思うと、当時の工作舎で一番欠けていた要素というのが、ファッショナブルな部分やどんな音楽を聴いているのかといったところにあったように思える。編集にとってその要素は不可欠なものだということを、松岡さんはもちろん知っていたはずで……。僕がその点について、どれだけのことを担えていたかどうかはわからないですけど、確実に評価してくれる人はいましたよ」

──確かにアカデミックなものやエスニックなものに対してはすごく強いけれども、オシャレな感じはしないという印象がありましたね。

デザインのスタイルについて

──ボクは、羽良多さんのようにスタイルを持ったデザイナーに憧れています。そのスタイルはどのようにして生まれたんですか?

「藤本さんは版下の時代を経験されているからわかると思うんですけど、真っ白な版下台紙を前にして、ロットリングだとか丸ペンで、まずはトンボの線を引くところから始まりますね。今では考えられないような仕事のスタイルですけど。要するにデザイン作業というのは一種のコラージュだった。コンテンツを1つの空間に収めていくという意味では、編集も同じかも知れませんね。そして問題はその収め方。そこにその人の身振り手振りがあるとするなら、それがスタイルと言えるのかな。そういうことなら僕は『HEAVEN』を折り返しに、今は最初のモノクロームな頃のデザインスタイルに戻っています。何か自分の内側にある自然の摂理にのっとっているような気分です」

──最初から『HEAVEN』のようなデザインスタイルだったわけではないんですか。

「そうですね。だから、あの頃のデザインを今見ると、近くて遠い感じがします。まったくテイストが変わってしまいました。今はもっと「白地」ということにこだわってデザインしています。というのも、もともと僕の中にはスイスグラフィックの流れがあったんです。高校時代に、何かの展覧会に行ってカタログを買う。でも、そのカタログのデザインが気に入らなかったりする。すると表紙に白なり黒の紙を被せて、そこにポスターカラーでレタリングをしたりして……。そのときの基本になっているデザインコンセプトが、スイスグラフィックだったんです。だから『HEAVEN』の頃のデザインとはかなり違っていました」

──もともとスイスグラフィックというモノクロームな根底が

あって、中間色のポリクロームな時代があり、今は"白"に戻っているということですか。そんなふうにドラスティックな変化はどうして起こったんでしょう。

「デザイン界がデジタライズされて、まだほんの数年しか経ってないでしょ。世界がデジタルに席巻されて、その喧騒が収まったのはほんの最近のこと。要するに、そのデジタライズされたフォントの大元はタイポグラフィーにあるから、スイスグラフィックも当然要素として入ってくる。それが僕にとってのきっかけになっているのかな。デジタライズという事件が、『HEAVEN』以前のデザインに自然に戻してくれたというか……」

手作業のドライブ感

──コンピューターグラフィックに移り変わって、何か変化はありましたか?

「それは変わりました。出来上がったものも含めて変わらざるを得ないですよね。可能性が広がるというよい方向だけではなく、現実と理想、両方のベクトルでの変化。特に今はハンドメイドのよさに戻るという流れが強いですね。その点『HEAVEN』を作業していた頃は、半分デジタル半分アナログ。僕にとってはそれが一番の理想の形です。というのも、やっていて非常にドライブ感がある。マシンだけでは充足感は少ないですよね」

──そもそもの話ですが、雑誌作りはお好きですか(笑)。

「こんなに面白いものはないですよ。いやいや、藤本さんがそんなこと言ってどうするんですか(笑)。要するに僕も藤本さんも、編集という概念に片足がどっぷり浸かっていますよね。デザインに編集という概念を持ち込むこと自体を、エディトリアルデザインと呼ぶのだと思います。そこまで広げないと面白くないんじゃないかな。しょせんデザイナーがどんなことを考えようと、情報は大きく分けると「テキスト」と「イメージ」。それをどう組み合わせていくか、足し算、引き算、かけ算、割り算、あるいは微分、積分して……。これをどうドライブしてくかということの面白さが、エディトリアルデザインには確かにありますよ」

　取材を終えて、羽良多さんは"才能の人"だと感じた。色彩のアイデアや構成力に並外れた才能を持っている。時代の空気などにはあまりとらわれず、自分の好きなスタイルを続けてきた人。そう言ったら語弊があるだろうか。それでもボクは彼の人柄やデザインから、彼にしか見えないイメージ、彼がずっと守ってきた特別な世界の存在を感じてしまう。

heiQuiti HARATA

Born 1947 in Tokyo. Graduated from Tokyo National University of Fine Arts and Music in visual design. Representative director of EDiX. Since 1970 in editing and producing *Shinjuku Play Map* and *Yu* (object magazine) and through his work on numerous magazines including *WX-raY*, *HEAVEN*, *GARO*, *Quick Japan*, *Japoneserie*, *Qui! La! La!*, and *TENGOCU_pixelzone*, Harata has been pursued the possibilities of editorial design by breaking new ground in publication design. He has also forged his own realm through collaborative work with the musicians YMO, Arico, and Yosui Inoue. Harata received the 1990 Kodansha Publishing Culture Award for Book Design for Taroupho Inaguaqui's novel *Issen ichibyo-monogatari* (Tale of 1001 seconds). He is a lecturer at Joshibi Junior College of Art and Design, and is currently envisioning a editorial design museum.

羽良多平吉

1947年東京生まれ。東京芸術大学美術学部工芸科V.D.専攻卒業。EDiX代表。1970年代より、『新宿プレイマップ』や『遊』の編集制作の他、『WX-raY』『HEAVEN』『ガロ』『クイック・ジャパン』『ジャポネズリ』『きらら』『点國』など、エディトリアルデザインの可能性を追究する書容設計の新境地を開拓。また、YMOやArico、井上陽水ら、音楽家への協力作業でも独自の世界を展開。1990年にイナガキ・タルホ著『一千一秒物語』(透土社)で講談社出版文化賞ブックデザイン賞受賞。女子美術短期大学造形学科デザインコース講師。現在、エディトリアルデザインミュージアムを構想中。

服部一成
KAZUNARI HATTORI

(here and there, 流行通信)
Ryuko Tsushin

Whether it's a large advertising campaign or a magazine, the viewer is always just one person.

It was in 2002 that Hattori Kazunari took on the redesign of *Ryuko Tsushin*. I had been in charge of art direction of the magazine until just before then and I thought his redesign was intellectual and beautiful. In style, it had a contemporary air and the graphics were full of his artistry. Now he works mainly in advertising while at the same time on the magazine *here and there*, published several times a year. In my mind, he embodies everything a graphic designer should be, but what is his approach to editorial design?

Advertising design and magazine design

— You're mainly involved in advertising at the moment, but how do magazine graphics compare with the graphics in advertising?
"They're different in various small ways. I was mainly doing advertising in my previous workplace, so the great difference in cycle and volume was hard-going. But strangely I had no sense of having to switch from one to the other. I had no choice but to just do it as I had always done. Actually what I've realized now is that you can't produce an entire magazine by yourself. In the case of advertising, I was obsessive about doing everything perfectly down to the last detail."

— There is always something that's not perfect, isn't there.
"I think some pages look rather good and there are others where I'm doubtful. However, I never feel like I should do away with the parts I'm not so keen on ... yes,

there is an unevenness, but for some reason, I think it works well ... it looks good. For me I suppose you could say it's been a learning curve. I feel as if I made some kind of breakthrough. I had a somewhat narrow way of thinking until then, I think. Of course I'm really involved and serious about what I do but at the same time I also need to be broad-minded to some extent."

Art direction that doesn't follow the rulebook

— Unlike advertising, magazines are produced by the people who buy advertising space and the editors. What do you think about that?"
"In the end, design is design, and a magazine has failed in its purpose if the editorial content isn't interesting. Because I had an interest in editing, I somehow ended up giving editing advice and I enjoyed it. When I think about it now, the reason I initially started doing design was that I was captivated by the merging of the words and the visuals. Because I was so concerned about the words side of it, I was reluctant to separate the editing of the articles and the design. So I ended up giving a number of headlines the thumbs down (laughs). There were of course many opportunities for me to learn things as well. As for the photos, I was confident from my experience in advertising work, and wasn't going to let myself be done by the editorial department, but there were things pointed out by editing that rather unexpectedly I hadn't noticed. Because I gradually began to feel confident about that, the result was that I was able to build good working relationships."

— Do you sometimes think, "Well, I took this approach in the previous issue so I think I'll change it for the next issue." What do you think of that kind of flow?

"When I'd been at the magazine about two years, the editor-in-chief and I had a meeting about special features planning and we made some decisions, and to some extent I was able to achieve some sense of balance by planning for the future. But I never really thought much about the flow of the design work. Each issue was going to stand or fall on its own merits so I thought it was better not to try and predict what was going to happen. In that sense, I think I had an amateur quality, someone who didn't necessarily follow a rule-book."

— There are of course methodologies in magazine design and I follow them in my design work, but your work on *Ryuko Tsushin* is completely different. Generally designers are methodical about readability and design flow but I can't see that with you. My image of you is someone who brings an artistic vessel and forcibly pushes contents into it. But that is really cool and fresh.

"I was initially unsure about the best way to approach things. I didn't really have that much an awareness of wanting to create my own style. The deciding factor was whether I liked something or not. Eventually I realized that was my direction. Going by what you like incorporates not only what's comfortable or positive but also a strange sense of incongruity. For example, when I design an ordinary magazine page, I let the content carry me along according to the theme, whether it's a European-style thing or a '60s thing. But I place limits on the typeface and color scheme and sometimes I don't even design according to a theme. That's how I manage to produce something like that sense of incongruity."

— What about differentiation from other magazines?"

"Of course I'm aware of it. But it doesn't make sense to design for the sake of differentiation. I tried not to forget the magazine's principle or the way things should be done. In the case of *Ryuko Tsushin*, that was probably because we didn't feel we needed to spoon-feed everything to our readership. In actual terms, we didn't feel we needed to go after something that was easy to read or easy to understand to that extent. Of course, compared with other magazines, we did have a feeling of wanting to stand out from the rest in absolute terms."

An awareness of mass-produced things

"I also really love printed media. Magazines too, the shelves of magazines in the bookstore, something cheap that anyone can buy. Lots of people just throw them away after they've read them, and there's something about them that I'm attracted to, maybe it's the fact that they're light or that they look cheap."

— I know what you mean. I also really like the feeling of the mass-produced.

"For example, very few people in Japan have heard of *here and there*, and when I think about that, compared with large advertising campaigns, I tend to think it's a really small medium, but then again I'm not sure. There are after all campaigns that appear to be presented in bold, splashy ways that don't stick in people's minds. Perhaps this is more a matter of even if only a few people see it, word gradually spreads, and then the number of people reading it grows.... So, even if it's something small, it fails if it doesn't reflect the desire to communicate to the reader or if it doesn't have that universality that's required when you produce something for the rest of the world. It's not about only doing the things that I want to do. Conversely, I don't like that shotgun way of some advertising campaigns. Whether it's a large advertising campaign or a magazine, the viewer is always just one person. In that sense, advertising and magazines are the same. For that reason, I think it's better not to compartmentalize things according to whether they're advertising or magazines or be conscious of their respective scale."

—You mean you're not consciously aware of any difference between your advertising work, *here and there* or *Ryuko Tsushin*?"

I really think I'm an amateur when it comes to magazine design. I can't tailor my approach to suit the medium I'm working in or be good at everything. Though there is something slightly pitiful about a design professional saying that there are things that he can and can't do (laugh). When I think about it now I guess I was just really into what I was doing then. I'd probably fail if I tried to do the same thing again. But I think at the time that part of me that wasn't quite sure whether I was doing the right thing but decided to do it anyway took the magazine in a good direction."

As I had thought, Hattori was a very self-effacing and hard-working graphic designer. I listened to what he had to say and I realized that the fact that he hadn't been aware of *Ryuko Tsushin* being a "magazine" meant that he'd created a new methodology for art direction. His design is shrouded in his innate artistic sensibility and he has suffused the magazine with the same atmosphere. I'm envious of that ability.

Ryuko Tsushin
流行通信

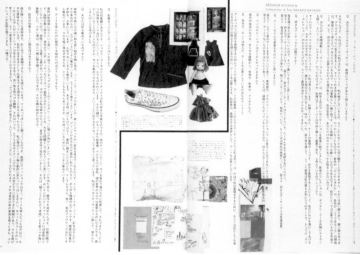

SONIA RYKIEL
PARIS

Ryuko Tsushin
流行通信

COLLECTION XC
女 性 上 位
CITIZEN

Her Clothes
Susan Cianciolo
Photograph TAKASHI HOMMA

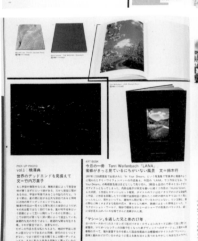

DESIGNER INTERVIEW
Composition & Text NAKAKO HAYASHI

MOVIE

TOPIC 文＝金原由佳
男子代？ 大洋ワールドの魅力

Fashion Check！ 文＝渡辺いく子
お馬鹿映画（＝クールで照れても脳をリセット）
文＝竹内万里子

PICK UP FILMS
文＝森直人

PICK UP PHOTO
vol.1 横澤高
今月の一冊＝ Terri Weifenbach 「LANA」
窓辺付きっと見ているにちがいない風景
文＝鈴木行

「ヴァーン」を過ごした亡と男の17年

ワキノシク・ポルノグラフィティ

ART

ART BOOK
TOKYO ART JUNGLE、雑誌感覚で探険を
文＝白須ゆり

Close up ヴィンセント・ギャロ レトロスペクティブ 1971-2002
動動のスッヴィンセント・ギャロの眼
文＝古川原真紀

FROM LONDON
ギルバート・ジョージの赤と黒
文＝清水和彦

GENKI
NEW YORK
New Photo Book
デニムの軌跡を一冊にまとめた「GENIUS」
文＝前田佳奈子

BOTANICA

TOKYO
Hot News
ナタリー・レテのキュートな商売アート

LONDON
New Shop
若手デザイナーの服を集めた、ひと味違うショップ
文＝坂本みゆき

FASHION

Culture Around This Month
さとうえこの
アンチ・ファッション・リポート
第3回 FASHION×FOOD
撮影・文＝佐藤絵子

ヴィンテージ・マガジン限定販売

FASHION
PARIS

ファーのストール

ティム・ヴァン・スティンヴァーゲンのネックレス

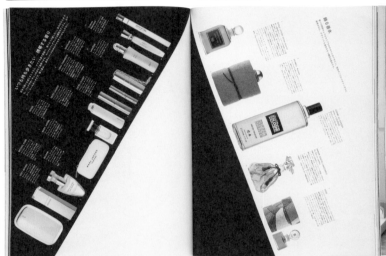

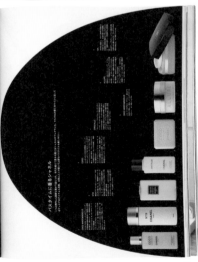

Alexander McQueen
アレキサンダー・マックイーン［ジョー・ストラマー］

JUNYA WATANABE COMME des GARÇONS
ジュンヤ ワタナベ コム デ ギャルソン［オムプラ］

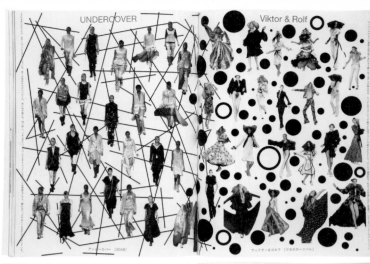

UNDERCOVER
アンダーカバー［SCAB］

Viktor & Rolf
ヴィクター＆ロルフ［リオのカーニバル］

COLOR CHART 2003 S/S

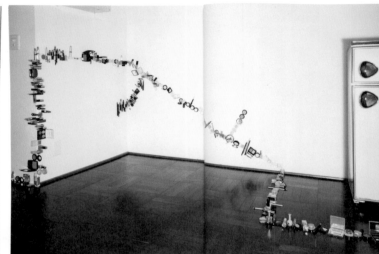

Photography MIKIYA TAKIMOTO

WARHOL LESSON

WARHOL LESSON

Chapter 2

TOPIC
WINKのカリフォルニア流「ポップ」　Photography WINK Text YUKI TAMURA

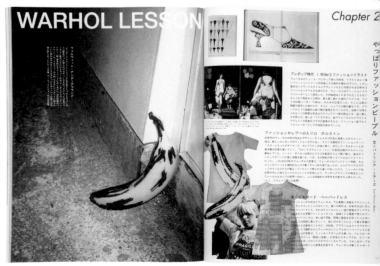

Chapter 6

Photography MIKIYA TAKIMOTO

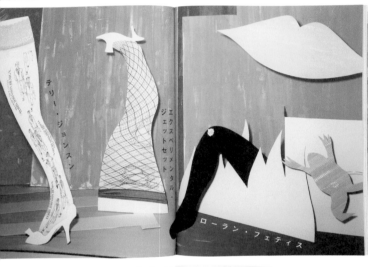

EDITOR'S CHOICE

LOOK

PICK UP

Styling FUSAE HAMADA

TREND
"ACTRESS"

LOOK

要チェックの会場演出

JIL SANDER　GUCCI　PRADA　MIU MIU　MILAN

大型ブランド×若手デザイナー　PERI

CHANEL　CELINE　Christian Dior

話題をよんだ展覧会　PARIS
Philippe STARCK　PAX
Karl face a Paris Lagerfeld　MILAN
ALBERTO RIZZO RETROSPETTIVA　alberto Rizzo

要チェックのプレゼン＆会場演出
COSMIC WONDER　ALEXANDER McQUEEN
Venera Arapu　Rochas

A　AOYAMA

Photography: TAKASHI HOMMA

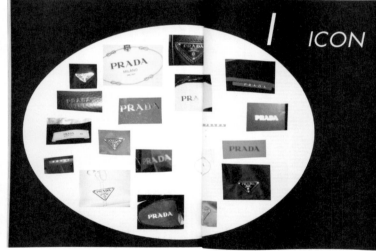

I　ICON

PRADA

P　PHILOSOPHY

特集：BOOK LIF

文学アルバム

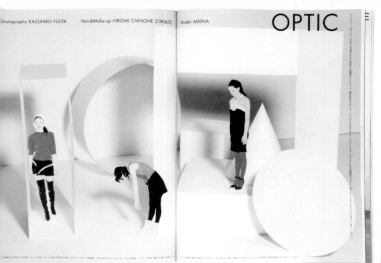

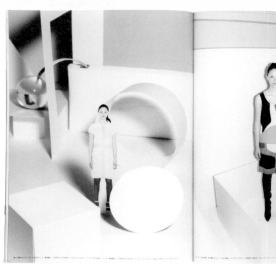

Photography KENSHU SHINTSUBO

Photography M.HASUI

shoes gallery

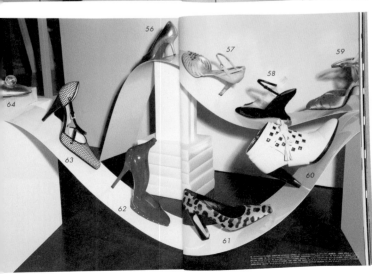

コズミックワンダーのシルバーパンプス

サルヴァトーレ フェラガモのオードリー

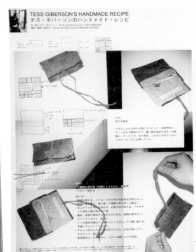

BJÖRK?

Photography NAOYA KIRAI

Photographer KAZUNARI HATTORI   Coordination MUTSUMI MORI   Special Thanks KEIJI ROSE NURSERIES, INC.

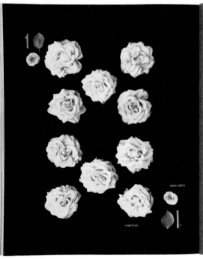

アルファベットライン

ALPHABET LINE by Christian Dior （シルエット傑作選・1）

ART DECO 〔アートとファッションの相関・1〕

ア
アール・デコ

シ
シュルレアリスム

SURREALISM 〔アートとファッションの相関・2〕

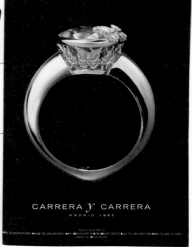

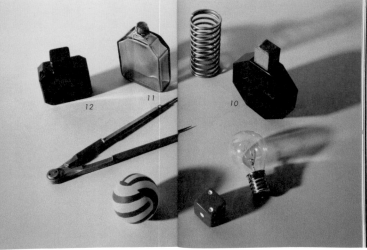

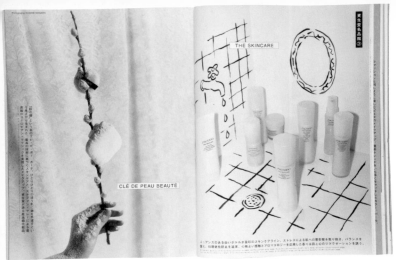

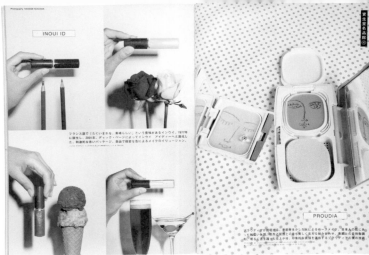

CLÉ DE PEAU BEAUTÉ

THE SKINCARE

INOUI ID

PROUDIA

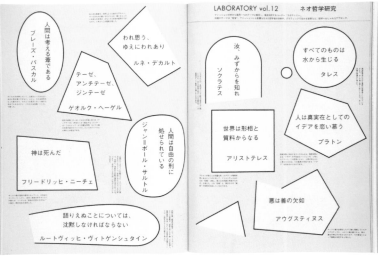

LABORATORY vol.12　ネオ哲学研究

人間は考える葦である
ブレーズ・パスカル

われ思う、ゆえにわれあり
ルネ・デカルト

テーゼ、アンチテーゼ、ジンテーゼ
ゲオルク・ヘーゲル

人間は自由の刑に処せられている
ジャン=ポール・サルトル

神は死んだ
フリードリッヒ・ニーチェ

語りえぬことについては、沈黙しなければならない
ルートヴィッヒ・ヴィトゲンシュタイン

汝みずからを知れ
ソクラテス

すべてのものは水から生じる
タレス

人は真実在としてのイデアを恋い慕う
プラトン

世界は形相と質料からなる
アリストテレス

悪は善の欠如
アウグスティヌス

OPTIC CLOTHES

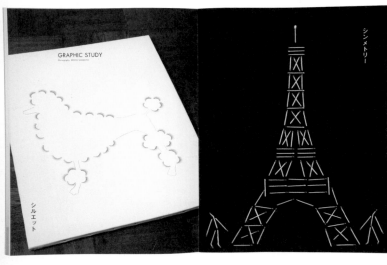

GRAPHIC STUDY

シンメトリー

シルエット

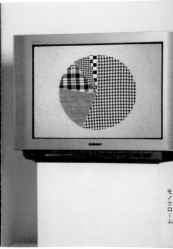

ネガとポジ

モノクローム

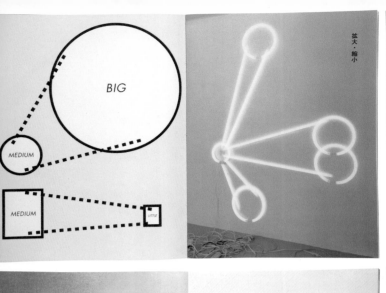

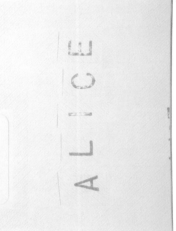

2002 AW Paris Collection Week Report

Cosmic Wonder
A Shadow Necessary for Windows
Palais de Tokyo

Marjan Pejoski　*Veronique Branquinho*

Ann-Sofie Back

Wendy & Jim

Antjelo Figus

Viktor & Rolf

Bernhard Willhelm　*Lutz*

here and there making diary
文・写真／林央子

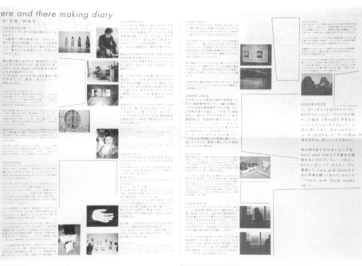

here and there fashion column 2

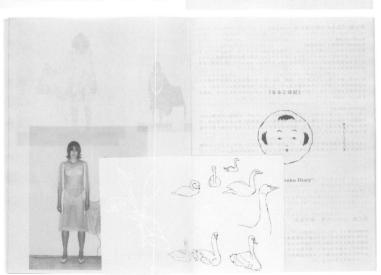

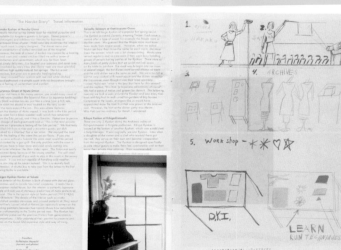

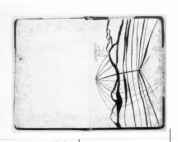

You are playing music in several bands now. Could you please tell me, the names of the bands, members of the band?	When did you start playing music? いつから音楽をはじめていたのですか?
yuki no shita Hisham - Mark, and Yuki and I in yuki no shita THE THIRD WAY Ariko and Yuki and I in THE THIRD WAY Also started playing with Maki in NY.	Started a few years ago; 4-5. But only very little- practicing on organ I had and electric base. I didn't consider it playing music, now begin to play more but still just playing very little. Feel shy about really talking about it. Look forward to play more.

Playing music requires different kind of concentration and creativity?

No, it is different way in letting go and expressing, am learning to find this.

Drawing, sewing and music. Can I say those three are the main activities for you now?

Yes and some business.
creating work - installations - performances

CONVERSATION WITH YUKINORI MAEDA, COSMIC WONDER
Text by Nakako Hayashi

Giving birth to my baby has changed my body, which made me out of my pre-baby clothes. So I visited the Cosmic Wonder boutique and got a pair of jeans. My life as a mom started with the jeans from Cosmic Wonder.

In the spring in Japan all sorts of entrance ceremonies are held so that town is filled with people in their brand-new clothes. For most of people, clothes are inseparable from their new life. Wearing the light blue jeans everyday I felt like thinking about 'Cosmic Wonder and the New Life.'

Q

The 2006 Autumn / Winter collection of Cosmic Wonder reproduced the clothes appeared in old pictures. And for the 06 Spring / Summer collection you started with questioning what is eternity and what is not, and presented clothes made of paper. Both collections each in a try to give new life to clothes to the non-clothes. How do you think about it?

A

Unexpected new life makes us happy. What Cosmic Wonder tries to do might be something like that.

Q

Now that you create new clothes in the world flooded with them, I think you're trying to make clothes with their own life. Is there anything you care for that?

A

And they have mysterious memories.

Q

Clothes are physical existence that won't have memories, but you create clothes that actually seem to have memories. You are like a magician, aren't you?

A

I think that is what WHITE MAGIC does.

SPECIAL 1
COSMIC WONDER ECLIPSE WEEPING ROCK

∞
MOSSLIGHT

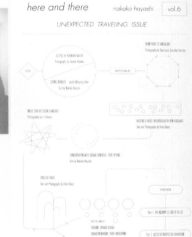

Text by Anne Daems
Translation by Anne Marie Poels, Nakako Hayashi.

Prelace

Last summer we visited Maison Lemoine, the house in Bordeaux designed by Rem Koolhaas. David Claerbout, an artist friend, and his filmcrew were shooting a film there during the month of July. This was the perfect occasion to go and visit this architectural icon. Initially we only wanted to pay a short visit and drive on to San Sebastian where Manifesta 5 took place, since we did not want to disrupt David's activities. But finally the visit developed at the one in 'The Magic Mountain' from Thomas Mann. In the novel Hans Castorp goes to visit his cousin in the sanatorium up in the mountains and ends up staying there for seven years. We drove up the mountain of Freine and stayed for three days and three nights. And as in Thomas Mann's novel, the house is a masterpiece. Of course the architect had the advantage of great conditions: an unique position with a view of Bordeaux, a mild climate that allowed for some Dutchism and employees with enough money and a sense of adventure. But it is also the way the house is insulated — with a lot of taste and a certain nonchalance — which makes it so special. An old tapestry with sketches from the Middle Ages serves as a curtain. It is accompanied by a camp from Achille Castiglione. A pastel in porcelaine and lots of beautiful vases next to the bed, an antique pink marble table in the kitchen and gladiolus from the curtain garden. Both Hélène Lemoine and her husband — who is deceased — pushed the architect to the extreme to insist on details to obtain the qualities the house has now.

Caview

The windows on the second floor, where both the bedrooms and bathrooms are located, are stroke. They have different sizes and allow you to have a look outside into several directions. Some have a golden frame and some are big enough to be opened. This creates intimacy and covers this light to be dimmed; wherever the gigantic windows in the living room and on the ground floor bring about the opposite. A pink element curtain draws a circle around Hélène's bed. A green, round lawn decorates the formal, eccentric inner yard, which is bordered by walls. In these walls a concrete, circular element can be opened. Outside the walls Hélène has cultivated a kitchen garden. The fig, tomatoes, eggplants, cucumbers, rosemary and lemon verbena are planted in two circles; a small inner circle and a bigger circle enclosing it. The lawn and the kitchen garden are the only two pieces of cultivated nature and everywhere else wild flowers growing abundantly in the premises and around the house. And last but not least there is a cylindrical, mirroring column with winding stairs, bearing the second floor.

Epilogue

Despite of the residents' knowledge of and interest in art, it is remarkable how sparingly it is present in the house. One enormous piece by Gilbert and George is integrated in the lift shaft, under a roof light. In the guestroom and in one of the bedrooms there are two sublime wallpaintings by Sol Lewitt. And recently Hélène also became owner of 'The Bordeaux Piece', the film David completed about the light in her house and about the time passing slowly on the magic mountain of Freine.

For Louise and Hélène, under the Bordeaux sun.
Anne Daems, September 9   2004, NYC.

here and there
nakako hayashi
vol.5 2004 winter
HOUSE AND GARDEN ISSUE

author Nakako Hayashi
art director Kazunari Hattori
http://www.nakakobooks.com

publisher Nakako Hayashi
c/o Muramoto 2-25-14 Ueda Setagaya
Tokyo Japan 156-00...
tel 81-3-3413-8205 fax 81-3-3413-8200
Distributor: Ricochet tel/fax 81-3-3804-3900
Designers: Kazunari Hattori, Nobuo Yamada, Mina Tabei
Translators: Kenichi Eguchi, Maya Nago, Mari Hagihara
©Nakako Hayashi 2004

9784902137750
1920071020006
ISBN4-902137-75-5
C0071 ¥2000E
定価(本体2000円+税)

BLESS N° 23 The bringer.

This seasons collection was co-designed by Caroline Melzig-Thiel and supported by the following interns: Hyomine Lee, Clarisse Soud, Lisa Spengler, Elizabeth Mackey, Elina Kellermann, Saskia Wendland, Christian Müller, Theresa von Meerveld, Christine Büschel, Yoko Mitsugishi, Johanna Lauren

BLESS has been awarded the prize 2004

Special thanks to the following companies and supporters:
ANGIOLANI, LOOPS, TIROS, ALSA THE SOLEMAKER, QUEI BRAVI RAGAZZI, ERREBI, GRAZZINA, BABY FRANCK & F Balfetti, INTIMARE, ICAS, BIEFFE, MODEL SERVICE, MEONI & CIAMPALINI, MILLET, INDUSTRIS DU CUIR, 52 Nord, DISCIPLE, BAUDELI IAN, ALAIN MIKLI, LA VOMATIK, ENSCI Les ateliers.

Ahle Pasqualin, Giuseppe Glono, Serenella Pasqualin, Xiaoqiu Lin, Family Sun, Family Lin, Anja Putzmann, Sigrid Henning, Jean Marie Midgeville, Jean Luc Guillemineau, Louis-René Bizners, Nathalie Dufour, Laurence Sudre, Miriam Stein, Madeleine Montaigne, Anna Flatz, Angelika Götz, Belkar & Jollet, Christina Jabs, Markus Wente, Madeleine Montaigne, Charly Gleize, François Brument, Yasmine Gauscher

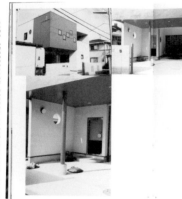

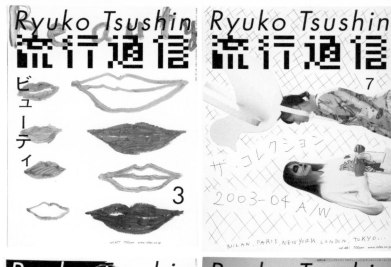

広告でも雑誌でも何でも見ているのは1人の人なんですよね

　服部一成さんが『流行通信』のリニューアルを手掛けたのが2002年のこと。直前まで同誌のアートディレクションを担当していたボクは、彼が手掛けた『流行通信』を見て知的で美しいと感じた。スタイルに今風の空気があり、アート性をグラフィックに落とし込む方法論があると。現在は、年に数回発行される『here and there』を手掛けるかたわら主に広告の分野で活躍している。ボクの中ではグラフィックデザイナーというイメージが強い彼だが、エディトリアルに対してはどういったスタンスでのぞんでいるのだろう。

広告デザインと雑誌デザイン

――現在は広告をメインにされていますが、いわゆる広告のグラフィックと比べて雑誌はどのように違いましたか？

　「細かいところではいろいろと違いますね。『流行通信』をやるまでは広告を中心にやっていたので、雑誌は時間のサイクルは早いしページ数は多いし、大変だと思いました。ただ、変に切り替えなきゃという意識はまったくなくて、結局自分にできるやり方でやるしかないなと。実際にやってみて感じたのは、雑誌は自分の意識で全部を作り切れないし、そこが面白さでもあるということです。広告の場合は、隅々まで完璧にやらなきゃという強迫観念みたいなものがありましたから」

――どうしても未完成の部分が残ってしまいますよね。

　「『なかなかいいな』と思えるページもあるけれども、逆に内容的に『どうなんだろう』というページもある。だけど、駄目な部分を全てなくしてしまえばいいわけでもない。凸凹はあっても、全体で見て魅力的に仕上がってればいいんだと考えるようにしま

した。僕としてはそれが勉強になったというか、何かふっきれた感じがありましたね。今までの考え方はちょっと狭かったなと。もちろんすごく入り込んで真剣に作り込むんだけど、同時に、駄目なところもあっていいという大らかな感覚も必要で」

雑誌の定石から外れたアートディレクション

――広告の仕事と違って、雑誌は発注側の人、編集者と一緒に作りますよね。そのあたりはどうでしたか？

　「所詮デザインはデザインにすぎないというか、編集内容が面白くなければやっぱり雑誌としては駄目ですよね。興味もあったから、編集にも口を出すようになっていって、それが面白かったです。もともとグラフィックデザインに惹かれたのは、今思うと、言葉とヴィジュアルが一緒になっているところだと思うんですよね。言葉の部分がすごく気になるから、記事は編集部、デザインはこっちと、きっちり分担してしまうのは面白くないと思っていました。記事のタイトルにダメ出しもしたし、僕が考えた見出しもけっこうありますよ(笑)。もちろん逆に教えてもらうこともいろいろありましたし、写真に関しては、広告でかなり経験してきたという自負もあったので、『編集部にわかるわけない』という気持ちがあったんですけど、意外と気付かなかった大切なことを編集部員から指摘されてなるほどと思ったりとか。そんなふうにだんだん忌憚なく言い合うという感じになっていったので、結果的にいい関係が築けたと思います」

――この手法は前号でやったから次は変えようとか、そういう流れについてはどうですか？

「だんだんと、特集企画を決める段階から僕と相談してというように編集部もなってきて、内容についてはある程度は先を見越してバランスを取っていました。でもデザインに関してはあまり流れを気にしないでやってましたね。表紙も含めて、毎号出たとこ勝負で、予測がつかないくらいの方がいいと思ってましたから。そういう意味では、雑誌デザインの掟からは外れた素人っぽさがあったと思います」

——やっぱり雑誌デザインにも方法論があって、そのやり方を踏襲しながらボクもやっているんですけど、服部さんの『流行通信』はまったく切り口が違うんですよ。普通は読みやすさや流れなんかを順序立てて進めていくんですけど、そういうものが見当たらない。ボクのイメージだと、アーティスティックな器を持ってきて、それにコンテンツを強引に押し込めているような感じ。でもそれがすごくかっこよくて新鮮でした。

「最初はどういうやり方がいいんだろうって迷いましたね。自分のスタイルで作ろうという意識はさほどなかったけど、自分が好きな感じというのはあるんですよね。だから結局はそこへ持っていこうとする。好きな感じというのは、心地よいとかきれいだとかいういい方向だけじゃなく、変な違和感具合とかも含めて。デザインが気が利きすぎてるのはどうも好きじゃない。例えば、普通誌面のデザインは、テーマに合わせてヨーロッパ調だとか60年代風だとか、内容に沿わせますよね。でもあえて書体や色を制限して、テーマとは無関係にデザインしたり。そうやって違和感みたいなものを出したりしてましたね」

——他の雑誌との差別化という点はどうでしたか？

「もちろん意識してました。でも差別化のためのデザインっていう考えではなくって、この雑誌の守るべき部分というか、こうあるべきだろうという部分を忘れないようにしてました。『流行通信』の場合、全ての読者に向けて全てを優しく作らなくてもいいんじゃないかということですよね。読みやすさやわかりやすさを多少犠牲にしても、なんかかっこいいとか、気になるとか、面白そうだとかいうことが大事だと思ってました。もちろん他の雑誌と比べて、絶対的に目立ちたいという気持ちはありましたけどね」

大量生産されるものに対する意識

「あとやっぱり、僕は印刷物というものがすごく好きなんです。雑誌も、普通に買える安いものとして書店に並んでいるところがいい。読んだら捨てちゃう人も多いし、その軽さというか安っぽ

さというか、そういう部分に惹かれるんですよね」

——よくわかります。ボクも大量生産の感じとか好きです。

「例えば『here and there』なんて日本全体で知っている人はごくわずかだし、そう考えると大きな広告キャンペーンと比べて、すごく影響力が小さいメディアと思ってしまいそうだけど、本当にそうかどうかは、よくわからなくて。実際、派手に展開しているように見えて、心に何も残らないものもありますよね。目にする人が少数でも、その人たちには確実に何かが伝わる、というものだったら、影響力が小さいとは言えないと思う。じわじわと広がっていくこともあるかもしれないし。だから、規模の小さいものでもただ自分が好きなことをやるというのではなく、ちゃんと相手に伝わるようにというか、世の中に通用する普遍性みたいなものがないと駄目なんだと思います。逆に大きい広告キャンペーンでも、大勢の集団にバーッと空からばらまく感覚でやっちゃうとまずいなと。大きいキャンペーンでも、雑誌でも何でも、見るときは1人の人がそれを見ているという状況は同じですよね。その意味では、広告だとか雑誌だとかの区別や、その規模なんかによってデザインを使い分けようとあんまり考えない方がいいと思う」

——広告の仕事でも『流行通信』でも『here and there』でも、あまり意識に差がないと……。

「雑誌デザインという点では、僕はアマチュアじゃないかと思うんです。それぞれの媒体に合わせたデザインとか、オールマイティには出来ない。出来るものと出来ないものがあるっていうのは、デザインのプロとしてちょっと情けないなっていう感じもありますけど(笑)。『流行通信』はうまくツボにハマってたんでしょうね。だけど、もう一回またこういう感じでやろうとすると、多分失敗すると思います。当時持っていた、『これでいいのかな』と不安に思いつつ『けどやっちゃえ』みたいな部分が、いい方向に出てた気がします」

　ボクの思っていた通り、彼はとても素直で一生懸命なグラフィックデザイナーだった。彼の話を聞いていて、"雑誌"であることを意識しなかったことが、逆に新しいアートディレクションの方法論を生み出したんだと感じた。彼のデザインには生まれ持った才能としてアートの気分が包み込まれていて、雑誌の中にもその空気感をサラリと吹き込んでしまう。そんなセンスにボクはうらやましさを感じてしまうのだ。

Kazunari Hattori

Born 1964 in Tokyo. Graduated from the design department of Tokyo National University of Fine Arts and Music in 1988 and joined Light Publicity Co., Ltd. He went out on his own in 2001. Among his broad ranging design activities are work on the revamping of *Ryuko Tsushin* (INFAS Publications) in 2002; advertising campaigns for Kewpie Half, East Japan Railway, and Laforet Harajuku; package design for Hotels Homes by Uniqlo; and book design on the Petit Royal French-Japanese Dictionary for Obunsha Publishing. Awards he has received include the Tokyo ADC Members' Award in 2003 and 2005, the Tokyo TDC Members' Award in 2004 and 2006, the Yusaku Kamekura Design Award in 2004, the Hiromu Hara Memorial Prize in 2005 and 2006, and the Tokyo TDC grand prix in 2007.

服部一成

1964年東京生まれ。1988年東京芸術大学美術学部デザイン科卒。ライトパブリシテイを経て、2001年に独立。2002年『流行通信』(INFASパブリケーションズ)のリニューアルを手掛けるほか、キユーピー「キユーピーハーフ」、JR東日本、ラフォーレ原宿の広告キャンペーン、ユニクロ「HOTELS HOMES by UNIQLO」のパッケージデザイン、旺文社『プチ・ロワイヤル仏和辞典』のブックデザインなど、幅広い分野で活躍。2003年2005年東京ADC会員賞、2004年2006年東京TDC会員賞、2004年亀倉雄策賞、2005年2006年原弘賞、2007年東京TDCグランプリなどを受賞。

JOP VAN BENNEKOM

(FANTASTIC MAN, RE-Magazine)

The ultimate designer doubling as editor
A form arrived at in the quest for personal expression

When *FANTASTIC MAN* magazine appeared, no one could not have been surprised by its audacious novelty. The first new kind of magazine to appear since the arrival of *Purple* around a decade earlier, everyone agreed that its editorial content was as fascinating as its visuals. For my part, I was amazed by the format of the binding, and frankly thought I'd never seen a magazine like it. The mastermind of *FANTASTIC MAN* is editor and art director Jop Van Bennekom. Jop first came to my attention with the likes of *RE-magazine* and *BUTT*, and on this occasion I traveled to Amsterdam to meet him for the first time. At his office on a peaceful canal, Jop confidently declared, "Magazine making for me is a mission. I don't want to sound arrogant, but I think I'm one of the few people making magazines without compromises."

A platform for personal expression

"Starting when I was about 16, I read lots of magazines and always wanted to create one. Just on 10 years ago in 1997, I launched my first: *RE-magazine*. I wanted to make a reality magazine in which I redefine communication. This was before the advent of reality TV shows like *Big Brother*. I wanted to document reality through my personal vision as directly as possible. Up until 2001 and the dot com crisis, there was an overflow of media, and people were looking for an alternative."

RE-magazine gained recognition shortly after its launch for its clear standpoint, personalized and original concept, and sophisticated design.

"Through doing *RE-magazine*, I learnt how magazines generally work and in 2001, together with Gert Jonkers, we launched a 'Fagazine', the *BUTT* magazine. *BUTT* is even more personal than *RE-magazine* and has a completely different style to other gay magazines. It's created a home for people, it's connected people, it's created its own world. As an editor that's the nicest consequence I could have asked for."

BUTT also brought a whole new visual aspect to gay magazines, with the use of pink paper, and its clean typography.

Then to *FANTASTIC MAN*

In 2005, *FANTASTIC MAN* was launched. As the subtitle, "Gentlemen's style journal", suggests, the art direction of the magazine is opposite to that of conventional glossy fashion magazines. With an uncoated cover, matt paper, and a lot of black and white photographs and textual pages, the magazine tells stories of "real" men with character and offers alternative and individual styles far removed from the glamour of the fashion world.

"The magazine has been going extremely well since its launch. A lot of *BUTT* readers also became readers of *FANTASTIC MAN*, so the magazine had a bit of a following to start with, but it then grew much bigger. We were rather surprised by the response, which has been especially good in America, plus Germany, France and England. It's not doing so great in Japan, maybe because there are lots of textual pages. Despite being a fashion magazine, we've included a lot of text-only pages. In a way, we are forcing people to read the text and if you don't read it, you don't get it. I've deliberately designed it to lead people to find out what the magazine's about through the text. *FANTASTIC MAN* is a fashion magazine with a journalistic approach and alternative viewpoints. It's my dream to see my magazine up there with *Vogue* and *Men's Health*. To create alternatives... "

Magazine making as a mission

Having launched three magazines, we asked Jop as an art director and editor what he thinks is required to make a magazine.

"It's not just one thing...but I see myself as a 'media person', not a graphic designer. And as a media person, I've always wanted to build new platforms for personal communication, and create the media I want. I think it's important to tell a different kind of story or possess different qualities to most magazines. And connect different kinds of people. Making magazines is like creating another kind of little world. It has its own universe. The way I see it, editing is very much my voice and it's like I'm always speaking to lots of people, and that's a very nice position to be in. And once you start making magazines, creating something that a lot of people feel comfortable with becomes very addictive."

The editorial-design connection

Jop has no interest in launching a web magazine. The choice of paper seems to be part of his uncompromising personal creativity.

"I love paper as an object and I think it makes more sense in 2007, where web magazines are so common, for printed magazines to have a very personal and physical feeling. Almost like touching your favorite garment...I think it's the right approach to magazines right now."

Although highly praised as a graphic designer as well as an editor, Jop doesn't take on commission work at all. Obviously, there is not much time left for other projects when he deals with everything from scratch, from devising the concepts for each issue, taking care of the business side, and writing articles, to small typographical details. If he has any inspiration or ideas he prefers to use them for the magazines.

"I like the fact that the editorial and the visual aspect of magazines always come together. So if you are an art director you are a bit of an editor and vice versa. Of course it's the editorial that comes first, no matter what. But the role of design I think is to ensure that in the end everything makes sense."

I began to think that the ultimate magazine designer might well be the editor. Jop is a rare example of this in practice. Talking to him however I realized he is not the slightest bit conscious of such things as the style of art direction. It's as if he set out on a quest to create the kind of world he would like, found a means of expression in magazines, then ended up an editor. His style is the completed form. But as a magazine designer, since meeting him I still keep thinking that perhaps there is another form.

FANTASTIC MAN

MR.
JONATHAN
ADLER

NEW YORK INTERIOR
DESIGN STAR IS KNOWN
FOR SPORTING
A VERY PARTICULAR
LOOK...

MR. ADLER

"WHEN I GREW UP I
TOTALLY DRESSED LIKE
A DORK. I HAD NO IDEA
WHAT TO WEAR"

HOUNDSTOOTH

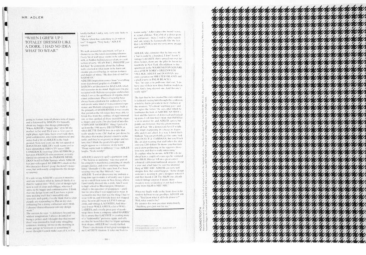

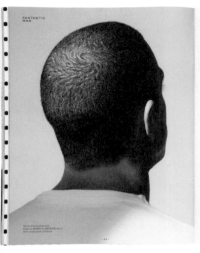

FANTASTIC MAN

T-SHIRT

After hitting a fashion zenith a few decades ago, the white T-shirt has since become inconsequential. But there's no doubt it's a classic; the clothing equivalent of a great haircut or marvellous pair of sunglasses. These days going out in a plain white T-shirt simply implies a quiet confidence, someone who doesn't need to be flash to feel good. Bring back the white T!

MR. CARLO

FANTASTIC MAN

COATS

COATS

HERRINGBONE

FANTASTIC MAN

AMANDA

MRS. AMANDA LEAR

SPARKS

Ron *Russell*

POP MUSIC'S MOST ECCENTRIC DUO
ARE CULT STARS IN EUROPE AND JUST TWO
ANONYMOUS BROTHERS IN LA...

SPARKS

Pop music is the place where eccentrics come out to play, and few have been as eccentric as SPARKS. The two brothers, RON and RUSSELL MAEL, along with an ever-changing array of collaborators ranging from GIORGIO MORODER to FAITH NO MORE, don't have just an instantly recognizable sound – courtesy of RUSSELL's bizarre falsetto and RON's equally out-there lyrics – they made sure to always look unforgettably great too. Having been welcomed and rediscovered over the years by the Brits, the French, the Germans, MORRISSEY, WARHOL and QUEEN, one could say they're a world-wide sensation, had it not been for the almost complete lack of recognition in their homeland, the USA. So be it – thanks to FRANZ FERDINAND, the brothers are right in the middle of another British SPARKS revival.

LA SILHOUETTE

The remarkable return of juxtaposed volumes and shapes...
drawings by PETER JEROENSE

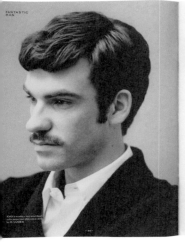

THE MOUSTACHE

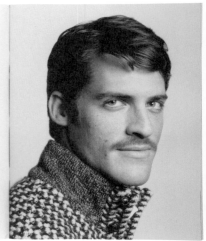

MISTER JOE
CASELY-HAYFORD

LONDON, ENGLAND

UTTERLY CHARMING
FASHION DESIGNER
HOPES TO TAKE THE ART
OF TAILORING INTO THE
21st CENTURY...

PHOTOGRAPHY – DAVID EVANS • STYLIST – SIMON FOXTON
TEXT – DEREK BRIGA

JERSEY

VOL.2
Mr. OLIVIER ZAHM

PARIS, FRANCE

THE RAVISHING
FRENCH LADYKILLER
LIVES FOR THE
NIGHT BUT WOULD DIE
FOR FASHION...

PHOTOGRAPHY – JUERGEN TELLER
TEXT – STEPHEN TODD

HELMUT

Mr. LANG may be the luckiest man alive. Since leaving his eponymous label in late 2004, the legendary designer has forged a radical new life for himself in the country. At his mid-century mark, he has his health, his wealth, his looks, his dogs and the love of a good man. And he is free.

WIM

Forty years ago, WIM CROUWEL was the Netherlands' unofficial chief designer. With his company TOTAL DESIGN, he created the graphic identity of just about every major Dutch cultural and commercial institution. From the Amsterdam STEDELIJK MUSEUM to the phone directory to the logo for the RANDSTAD employment agency, his aesthetic was impossible to avoid. Restricting his design palette to a handful of grids and two sans serif typefaces (UNIVERS and HELVETICA), CROUWEL rendered Holland the most visually consistent of all nations. By his own admission, he was a dogmatist: several times during our afternoon's conversation he cups his hands around his eyes to illustrate the blinkered nature of his erstwhile vision. If he says so it must be true, but it is hard to reconcile the gracious, open-minded, loose-limbed, seventy-something Mr CROUWEL, with this image of a stubborn hard-liner. These days, the designer harbours a more flexible approach and a passion for fast cars – although he's still not sure about FRANK GEHRY.

MONSIEUR
BENOÎT
DUTEURTRE

PARIS, FRANCE

THE CHARMING
FRENCH WRITER AND
THE DYING EXPERTISE OF
'STYLE NÉGLIGÉ'...

PHOTOGRAPHY – MERCUS BEISS
TEXT – BRIAN HENDERSON

CHAUSSURES

THIS PAGE:
PILATI wears a black and white twin-pieced silken coat by YVES SAINT LAURENT PARIS...

PREVIOUS PAGE:
Armoured Vest by CHRISTIAN LACROIX
poplin shirt and woollen trousers by YVES SAINT
LAURENT RIVE GAUCHE. Bag by PRADA.

MR. STEFANO
PILATI

THE INCONGRUITY OF SUITS AND SURFING FITS THE ECCENTRIC DESIGNER OF YVES SAINT LAURENT PERFECTLY WELL...

PHOTOGRAPHY — INEZ VAN LAMSWEERDE & VINOODH MATADIN   INTERVIEW — TIM BLANKS

"I don't want to focus my energy on youth. I want to focus it on someone who can feel it."

LOOK: A grey Lightweight cotton jersey shirt by PAUL SMITH, trousers worn only by STUSSY and shoes worn by MIU MIU

Main: POLO SHIRT in blue
by the SCOTT at Dunhill
Trousers by MICHAELIS

PLEATS

PLEATS ARE A FORGOTTEN LUXURY THAT THOUGHT SUPPLEMENTAL & CONVENTIONAL DOUBLE PLEAT INCREASES THE WIDTH OF TAKING IN A PAIR OF TROUSERS BY AT LEAST 1CM. HERE REHAB TO BRING PLEATS BACK INTO THE FOLD. — BY JEFFS ANDERSON

NEW YORK

Once a freelance journalist who co-founded the futuristically monikered BIOMATRIX biotech company with his Dad and made a fortune when it went public, the world now knows Mr ANDRÉ BALAZS as the master-mind behind the complete transformation of LA's seedy, run-down CHA-TEAU MARMONT hotel into one of Hollywood's most fabulous address-es. He quickly followed with THE MERCER, the STANDARD HOTELS and a handful of other local yet absurdly influential projects. In a way, Mr BALAZS is one of those people who has defined the aesthetic of the world that we live in today. Although his natural habitat is among celebri-ties, he claims not to be one himself. In fact, there's an unexpected shy-ness about him which belies his recurrent PAGE 6 visibility. Mr Balazs lives in New York, but he's never home, of course.

LE CRÉATEUR

TRÈS PARISIAN...
LANVIN'S MENSWEAR DESIGNER LUCAS OSSENDRIJVER PROMENADES HIS LATEST COLLECTION

PLACE VENDÔME

PHOTOGRAPHY — DANIEL RIERA   STYLIST — JONATHAN KATZ   TEXT — GLENN WALDRON

Mr. DAVID BAILEY
— LONDON —

THE BRUTAL HONESTY AND WICKED CHARM OF THE LEGENDARY BRITISH PHOTOGRAPHER...

PHOTOGRAPHY — WERNER FELLER   TEXT — TIM BLANKS

SHIRT

A PERFECT WHITE SHIRT — DEFINITIVELY NOT A SHAPELESS DEPARTMENT STORE GARMENT, BUT A REFINED PIECE OF UNDERSTATED DESIGN

PHOTOGRAPHY — MAURICE SCHELTENS
FASHIONS STYLIST — JAIME GONZALO   SET STYLIST — LIESBETH ABBENES
TEXT — MATTHEW CULERWO

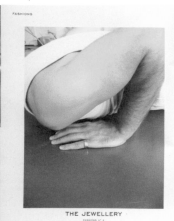

THE JEWELLERY

MR. TURIN

THE PHANTASMAGORICAL PERFUME CRITIC AND BIOPHYSICIST IS A MAVERICK AMONG SCIENTISTS AND SCENTS...

THE MANNEQUIN

HERE COMES THE SUN

BY WOLFGANG TILLMANS

THE SUN

THE RECOMMENDATIONS

RECOMMENDED BY STEPHEN TODD

TAKING A BREAK FROM WINTER WHERE IT'S SUMMER

RECOMMENDED BY PETER JENSENS

THE SHAPELESS, COLOURLESS, FUSSLESS LOOK FOR A RELAXING EFFECT

AARON

Mr. AARON DE MEY from NEW YORK CITY, make-up artist, modelling HIMSELF for Issey van Lamsweerde & Vinoodh Matadin, page 33...

FANTASTIC MAN

MR. THOM BROWNE,
THE PHOTOGRAPHER,
MR. MALCOLM McLAREN,
TWEED,
MR. RUPERT EVERETT,

THE DANCER,
MR. DENNIS FREEDMAN,
THAT CAMERA,
DELIGHTFUL PYJAMAS,
MR. ROY BLAKEY,
WONDERFUL MEN,

MR. MALCOLM

McLAREN

THE QUINTESSENTIAL ENGLISHMAN IN PARIS MIGHT TAKE HOLLYWOOD, BERLIN AND MILAN BY STORM WITH SOME BLOODY INTERESTING NEW PROJECTS...

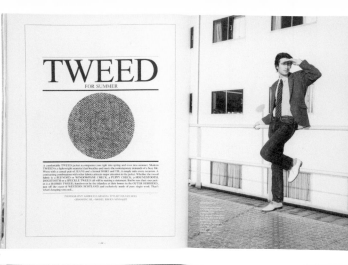

TWEED
FOR SUMMER

A comfortable TWEED jacket accompanies you right into spring and even into summer. Modern TWEED is a lightweight material that breathes and meets the contemporary demands of a busy life. Worn with a casual pair of JEANS and a formal SHIRT and TIE, it simply suits every occasion.

MR.
RUPERT
EVERETT

UTTERLY CHARMING FILM STAR HIDES IN MIAMI TO WRITE MEMOIR...

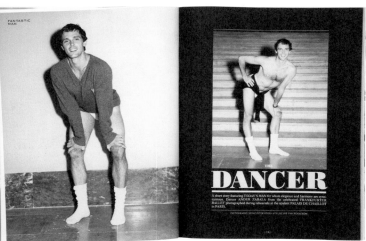

MR. FREEDMAN

DENNIS is the man who's made the pages of inimitable fashion mag W worthy of their own gallery at MoMA. His pioneering concepts for the magazine have given other consumer rags a challenge they have yet to meet. The HUNT for great talent is something Mr. FREEDMAN is well known for in both his professional and private life. DENNIS is an esteemed collector of MODERN FURNITURE, DESIGN and PHOTOGRAPHY, yet his house resembles a haphazard museum archive, quite different from its chocolate box exterior...

THE DANCER

A short story featuring TODAY'S MAN for whom elegance and harmony are synonymous. Dancer ANDER ZABALA from the celebrated FRANKFURTER BALLET photographed during rehearsals at the opulent PALAIS DE CHAILLOT in PARIS.

WONDERFUL
MEN

For decades, photographer ROY BLAKEY celebrated the male nude in his steamy CHELSEA studio. His resplendent images of men graced both arty AFTER DARK and raunchy HONCHO, not to mention his 1972 cult classic coffee table book HE. As one can see, being naked is nothing but an attitude...

FANTASTIC LIFE

FANTASTIC COLOUR

1997 SO 2005 DATED 1984

INTRO-DUCING JOHN

Photography Martine Stig

ONE QUESTION INTERVIEW

Q: WHO ARE YOU?

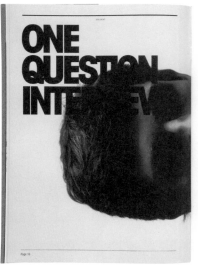

A: JOHN

PART ONE

Epilogue.

VERY EXTENSIVE NOTES AND CREDITS :

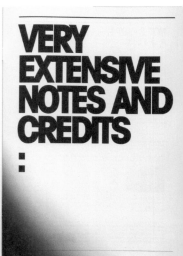

— FORMAT : CONTENTS —

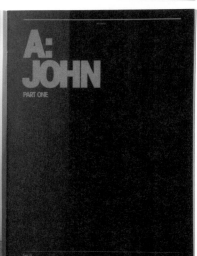

ISSUES.

— FORMAT : CONTENTS —

(...)
Re-Magazine #7

— NOT IN THIS ISSUE —

— NOT IN THIS ISSUE —

— FORMAT : REVIEW —

Hysterical Smoke.

Hello.

— Selected Writings —

"Mathematical Spectacle."

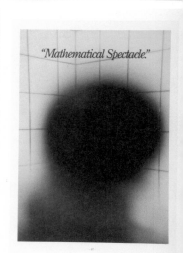

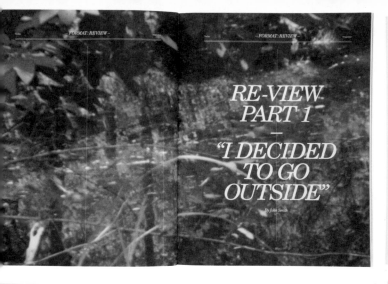

RE-VIEW. PART 1
—
"I DECIDED TO GO OUTSIDE"

By John Smith

Short.

A LONG STORY SHORT

by Lemuel Engelberts

MAIL TO: CLASSIFIEDS@LOSTBOYS.COM

"FADE TO CLAY"

Re-Magazine

Interview.

LONG INTERVIEW.
BORING.
NEUROTIC.
DISAPPOINTED.
HORRIFIED.
UGLY.
COMPETITIVE.
BITTER.
DEPRESSED.

Series.

MOOD SWINGS.
IN LONDON.
STEREOTYPES.
THERAPY.
EXHAUSTED.
BACK TO THE OLD HOUSE.

Plus.

REALITY CHECK.

'An eight hou-r long interview with Hest-er.'

One.

Hester lives in a modest two room flat in a converted factory in London.

Did you come up with an answer?

'N-EUROTI-C.'

"Neurotic women drive me up the wall. I can't stand it. It's hard work being around neurotic people. A display of neuroticism makes me neurotic as well."

I simply can't stand being on the tube. It's a claustrophobic experience to be trapped in a capsule and push through a tunnel.

I'm VERY sensitive to spaces. I hate being locked up in a small room.

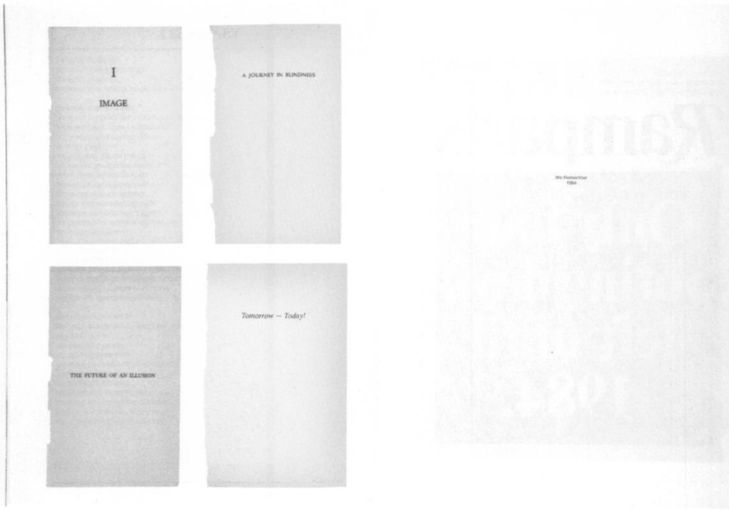

I
IMAGE

A JOURNEY IN KINDNESS

Tomorrow — Today?

THE FUTURE OF AN ILLUSION

THE INFORMATION TRASHCAN

Advertisement.

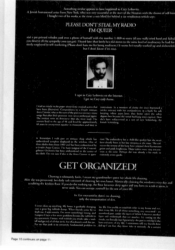

adidas
FOREVER SPORT

Page 2 continues on page 3.

No page.

Not.

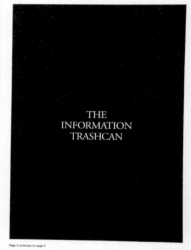

DUST

I = SELF EXPRESSION

Page 9 continues on page 10.

PLEASE DON'T STEAL MY RADIO
I'M QUEER

GET ORGANIZED!

Page 10 continues on page 11.

No page.

SICK!

I = COKE

Not.

SICK!
STRAWBERRIES
SICK!

Not.

Page 12 continues on page 13.

No page.

I DIDN'T GO TO WORK TODAY... ...I DON'T THINK I'LL GO TOMORROW

LET'S TAKE CONTROL OF OUR LIVES AND LIVE FOR PLEASURE NOT PAIN

Page 22 continues on page 23.

THE AIDIES

DOWN WITH ME!

DOWN WITH ME!

Page 23 continues on page 24.

Page 27 continues on page 28.

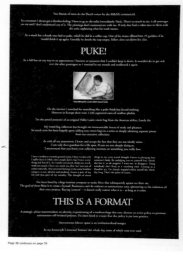

PUKE!

THIS IS A FORMAT

Page 28 continues on page 29.

No. – Contents.

No. 1 Family.

Re-connect attempt No. 1
Family.
Re-connect with your roots.
Go and live with your parents again.
An interview with Tanja who did.

Text: Arnoud Holleman.
Photography: Thomas Manneke.

Family.

Family.

No. 2 Neighbors.

Re-connect attempt No. 2
Neighbors.
Re-connect with neighbors you don't know.
Visit your neighbors, introduce yourself.
Hi, it's me!
Text: Jop van Bennekom/Lernert Engelberts.
Photography: Misha de Ridder.

Ms. 47-f

Ms. 47-c

No. 3 Surroundings.

Re-connect attempt No. 3
Surroundings.
Re-connect with everything that surrounds you.
Let's get physical.
Photography: Elspeth Diederix.

Surroundings.

Surroundings.

No. 5 Mother.

Re-connect attempt No. 5.
Mother.
Re-connect with your mother.
Explain yourself, show her your work.
Meet your mother.

Text: Lennart Engelberts/ Gisbert van der Wal.
Fotografie: Marian Goossens/ Misha de Ridder.

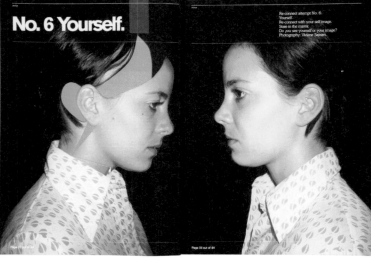

Mother.

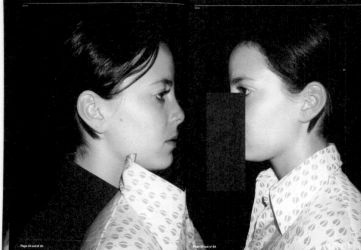

This is a work of art. To your left: a monitor shows the heavily made-up face of a Chinese girl in close-up. She gazes at you sadly for a few seconds. Then a handful of cooked rice is thrown in her face. The girl fights to keep a straight face as the gobs of sticky rice fall off one by one.

No. 6 Yourself.

Re-connect attempt No. 6.
Yourself.
Re-connect with your self-image.
Stare in the mirror.
Do you see yourself or your image?
Photography: Viviane Sassen.

Re-connect attempt No. 7
Past.
Those good old days you shared with friends.
Friends you now share only sweet memories with.
Text: Guus Beumer

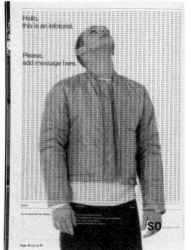

Hello,
this is an infotorial.

Please,
add message here.

Adolescence.

I saw you in a magazine..

May we help you?

Lufthansa

No. 9 Media.

Re-connect attempt No. 9
Media
Re-connect with an old issue of National Geographic.
Say hi to a face in the magazine.
Strike up a conversation.
Text: Jop van Bennekom

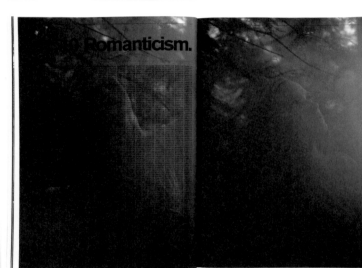

0 Romanticism.

No. 11 Friend.

Re-connect attempt No. 11:
Friend
Re-connect with your best friend.
Show a real interest, just ask why, why, why?
Jop van Bennekom interviewed Karin
Photography: Misha de Ridder

Why text?

Why picture?

No. 12 Strangers.

Re-connect attempt No. 12
Strangers
Re-connect with strangers called Friend.
Call a friend in order to make a new friend.
Let's play Friends!
By Jop van Bennekom, Yemen Engelbarts.

Vri

Hello,
this is an infotorial.

Please,
add message here.

Lost Boys

Last Attempt

No. 13 Network.

Network.

No. 1 Family.

Family.

Contents

Bored!

Colophon:

Editorial:

'Like'... awareness

Talkin'around...

Hello, This is an advertisement.

FreeStylin' Looking at forms of boredom. Creating clouds of text.

編集長を兼任した究極のデザイナー
自分の表現を追求した結果、辿り着いた形

　『FANTASTIC MAN』が登場したとき、誰もがその新しさに驚いたはずだ。『Purple』以降、約10年振りに登場した新しいタイプの雑誌で、編集内容もかなり興味深いというのが皆の評価。一方ボクはといえば、その造本形態に衝撃を受け、"今までに見たことのない雑誌だ"というのが率直な感想だった。手掛けているのは編集長とアートディレクターを兼任するヨップ・ファン・ベネコム。もともと『RE-magazine』や『BUTT』の頃から注目していた人物で、今回初めて彼に会うためにアムステルダムを訪れた。静かな運河沿いにあるオフィスで、「雑誌作りは僕の使命。自慢じゃないけど、これほど妥協なく雑誌を作っている人は稀だと思う」と彼は自信に満ちた口調で語り始めた。

パーソナルな表現のプラットフォーム

　「16歳の頃から雑誌が大好きで、ずっと雑誌を作りたいと思っていました。今からちょうど10年前の1997年に作ったのが、最初の雑誌『RE-magazine』。きっかけは自分が捉えた日常を記録し、コミュニケーションを再定義したいと思ったから。いわゆるリアリティをテーマにした雑誌にしたかったんです。今となってはそういうテレビ番組がブラウン管の中で現実になっているけれど、僕がやりたかったのは、身の回りの日常をできるだけ真実に近い形で切り取ること。また、2000年頃まではインターネットによるバブル経済が続いていて、メディアは飽和状態。みんなが新しいものを求めていたという状況もあると思います」

　『RE-magazine』はその明確な立ち位置、私的なコンセプトの独自性やデザインの洗練性により、立ち上げてすぐに注目を集めることになる。

　「『RE-magazine』で、ある程度、雑誌作りのノウハウを学んで、2001年にゲルト・ヨンカースとともに『BUTT』を立ち上げました。『BUTT』は『RE-magazine』よりもさらに個人的な内容で、今までになかったスタイルのゲイ雑誌です。この本が、自分の拠

り所を見つけるきっかけになったり、人と人を繋ぐ橋渡しになったり、『BUTT』特有の世界が確立されたと言えますね。これは編集者として一番うれしいことだと思います」

全ページにわたってピンク色の紙を使用したり、クリーンなタイポグラフィーを使ったりと、それまでのゲイ雑誌の流れからするとヴィジュアル面でもまったく新しい手法が見られた。

『BUTT』から『FANTASTIC MAN』へ

2005年に『FANTASTIC MAN』を創刊。"メンズスタイルジャーナル"というサブタイトルが示すように、既存のファッション誌とは異なる編集内容、そしてそのアートディレクションは見事だった。マット紙使いやモノクロ写真の多用など、彼独自のスタイルを開拓したという印象が強い。
「『FANTASTIC MAN』は、想像以上に反応がよくて、正直驚きました。『BUTT』の読者がそのまま『FANTASTIC MAN』を読んでくれているという場合もありますが、新たな読者もかなり増えました。欧文テキストの多さから日本ではそれほど売れていないようですが、アメリカやドイツ、フランス、イギリスなどで特に好評なんです。

『FANTASTIC MAN』では、ファッション誌であるにも関わらず、テキストのみのページを多くしました。読者にしっかり記事を読んでほしいという意図から、一見しただけでは内容がわからないページがたくさんあります。記事が一番引き立つようなデザインと言えますね。メンズファッションを切り口に、ジャーナリスティックな新しい視点を提案することをコンセプトにしています。自分の雑誌が『Vogue』や『Men's Health』といった雑誌の隣に、選択肢として並べられるのが夢ですね」

使命としての雑誌作り

オリジナルの雑誌を3種も世に送り出してきた彼は、アートディレクターとして編集者として、雑誌作りには何が必要だと思っているのだろう。
「いろいろな要素がありますね。僕は自分のことをデザイナーではなく"メディア人間"と思っていて、その立場から、個人的なコミュニケーションの基盤を築き、自分が欲しいと思うメディアを作りたいとずっと考えてきました。大切なのは人と違うス

トーリーを描き、他の雑誌とは違うクオリティを持つこと。さらに、型にはまらないで人々を繋ぐことも大事だと思います。そして、それが新たな世界を創り出すことにつながると信じています。僕の場合、とても個人的な内容の雑誌を作っているのに、自分の意見に賛同してくれる読者が世界中にいると思うと、すごくいい立場ですね。そういったことを含めて、一度、雑誌作りを始めると、癖になってやめられなくなります」

編集とデザインの関わり

ウェブマガジンの開拓にはまったく興味がないという彼。使用する紙も、クリエイションの重要な一部と考えているようだ。
「ウェブマガジンが一般的に出回っている今、あえて紙媒体にこだわるのはとても大事なことだと思います。お気に入りの生地に触る心地よさを味わうように、紙に触れるということ自体が素晴らしいし、また紙にこだわることによって、触れるだけで雑誌によって違う感触を味わうことができるのは、すごく"今"らしいと思うんです」

デザイナーとしても定評のあるヨップだが、雑誌以外の仕事はやらないそうだ。経営から原稿書き、コンセプト作りからタイポグラフィーのディテールに至るまで、全てを統括している彼には、他のプロジェクトに費やす時間が残らない。また彼自身、思いつくアイデアやインスピレーションは全て雑誌に捧げたいと語る。
「雑誌作りの面白いところは、さまざまな役割が繋がっているところ。例えばアートディレクターが編集に携わったり、編集がデザインに関わったり。編集が常に軸にならなければいけないけれど、最終的につじつまが合うように上手くまとめあげるのがデザインの役割だと感じています」

常々ボクは究極の雑誌デザイナーとは編集長なのかもしれないと感じてきた。ヨップはそれを成し遂げている希有な例と言える。でも、彼に話を聞くとアートディレクションのスタイルなんて、まるで意識していなかった。自分の好きな世界を追求していくと、そこに雑誌という表現があって、編集長という席があった、という感じ。彼のスタイルは完成された形だと思う。だけど、雑誌デザイナーとして、また別の形があるのではないかと、彼と会った後もボクは考え続けているのだ。

Jop Van Bennekom

Launched RE-Magazine in 1997 after graduating from Jan van Eyck Academie in Maastrichit, Holland. During this time he also worked for a year as art director of Blvd. and designer of the architecture magazine Forum. In 2001 he launched the gay magazine BUTT together with journalist Gert Jonkers, working as art director, designer, writer, stylist, and publisher, and in 2005 again with Gert Jonkers, "the gentlemen's style journal" FANTASTIC MAN, which soon become the talk of the world.

ヨップ・ファン・ベネコム

1997年、オランダ、マーストリヒトのヤン・ファン・アイク・アカデミーを卒業後、雑誌『RE-Magazine』を立ち上げる。その間、『Blvd.』のアートディレクター、建築雑誌『Forum』のデザイナーも1年間務める。2001年、ジャーナリストのゲルト・ヨンカースとともにゲイ雑誌『BUTT』を創刊。編集者、アートディレクター、デザイナー、ライター、ストラテジスト、出版社の全てを手掛ける。2005年、同じくゲルト・ヨンカースとともに"ジェントルマンズスタイルジャーナル"といううたい文句のファッション雑誌『FANTASTIC MAN』を立ち上げ、世界中で話題となる。

M/M(Paris)

(VOGUE PARIS)

Artistic form blowing a fresh breeze through magazine design

You can tell what kind of art director a person is by looking at their workplace: as in this person obviously leans toward the business side of things, for example, while this one is more of an artist. When I visited the offices of M/M (Paris) and found a place with the ambience of a painter's studio, I knew my premonition was correct: observing their work, I'd noted that they always seemed to have one foot in the domain of the artist. For two years starting in 2002, they worked on *VOGUE PARIS*. A few years on, their reputation as artists has grown immensely.

Designers and artists

"We've viewed ourselves as designers but at the same time artists right from the beginning. Recently I think the art world has also started to recognize us as such."

To be honest, I must confess that when I first saw *VOGUE PARIS* when they were responsible for it, I didn't rate their work very highly. Right from back then of course, the innovativeness of their design techniques and determination to try things nobody else had ever attempted were obvious, but from a magazine design perspective, their work was a little rough and ready in certain respects. Looking back I can identify signs then that they would go on to establish themselves as artists.

Magazines produced by M/M (Paris)

Following their work for *VOGUE PARIS*, the pair were invited to work as guest art directors on various magazines, including *i-D* and *V magazine*. If they were to become the editors of their own magazine, what kind of magazine would they produce?

"After we quit working for *VOGUE PARIS* we received a lot of offers from fashion magazines such as *i-D*, *Purple Fashion*, *V magazine* and *W magazine*. Usually when magazines choose an AD they pick someone with a connection to the magazine publisher, however they sought us out even though they were not from the publishers of *VOGUE PARIS*.
Thus we've been involved in all sorts of subject matter through our magazine work: rock culture at *Les Inrockuptible*, house and club music at *eDEN*, contemporary art at *Documents sur l'art* and *Frog*, clubbing culture at *Wow*, fashion at *VOGUE PARIS*... And now we've been appointed creative directors for *Arena Homme Plus*. At the moment we're very satisfied with our work."

Arena Homme Plus is thus the latest publication to be designed by this pair with their extensive magazine experience. So this time, will they follow the conventions of magazine design, or pour their art into the magazine? One thing is certain: they will offer an exciting new design style.

After *Arena Homme Plus*

"If we're to do any more magazines, it would be interesting to do a magazine that didn't need to be up-to-the-minute contemporary, and that in a way had lost its spark. A lot of magazines like that only survive as the object of advertising campaigns, and many wouldn't touch that kind of job. But reworking a magazine like that into something interesting would be a fascinating challenge."

Having worked on *VOGUE PARIS* and *Arena Homme Plus*, no doubt they will continue to blow a fresh breeze through the world of magazine design. Tokyo and Paris may be 10,000km apart, but having observed the M/M approach to magazine design, I can't help feeling I know them intimately.

"Those two years were a really intense time for us. Once we'd been put in charge, we started by promptly overhauling the design of the whole magazine, and took six months to rebuild the content, redefine the magazine's message, and remake the visual language. Once all these elements were in place it was a smooth process to alter the final design. We went for a classic look, one that gave the magazine a finished form utilizing the best we had to offer. The practical design tasks were performed in a short space of time, during which we transformed *VOGUE PARIS* into a kind of movie star of the fashion world. Mind you, obviously we were under a lot of pressure to get results."

Affichage sauvage.

Alice dans les îles

En tenue d'Eva...

Prête à tout

Le grand jeu.

Le jean.

Photographe MIKAEL JANSSON
réalisation ANASTASIA BARBIERI

Perdue dans Manhattan.

Quand la féminité glacée des années 50 erre dans la jungle en béton d'aujourd'hui, la grâce savoie la solitude des grandes villes. Restent les volutes d'une silhouette envoûtante au tournant d'un parc, les phares d'un taxi et quelques gouttes de pluie.

Propos recueillis par OLIVIER LHANNE
photographie GUY BOURDIN

Badinter, l'autre féminisme.

Philosophe et historienne, Élisabeth Badinter a toujours accompagné le combat des femmes pour l'égalité, convaincue du primat de la culture sur la nature. Après avoir remis en cause l'instinct maternel (*L'Amour en plus*), un affirmé la ressemblance des sexes (*L'un est l'autre*), elle condamne aujourd'hui dans *Fausse Route* (Odile Jacob) les dérives du féminisme des quinze dernières années. Rencontre.

« J'espère qu'on va se lever le tabou et travailler sur la violence féminine, un terrain encore à défricher pour mieux connaître les deux sexes. » **Élisabeth Badinter**

« J'ai le sentiment que les jeunes hommes, non seulement ne savent plus à quoi ils servent, mais qu'eux aussi sont traités comme des objets par les filles. » **Élisabeth Badinter**

Par MARIE DOSVENTURIER

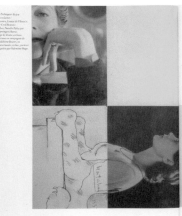

Par CLAUDE ARNAUD,
illustration LAURA BALLIS.

Les femmes de Cocteau.

« Poète de la poème des images jusqu'au bec de la plume », comme l'écrivait Morand, Jean Cocteau fait les honneurs de la rentrée : une exposition au Centre Pompidou ainsi qu'une biographie captivante signée Claude Arnaud. St Cocteau, dont l'œuvre est essentiellement tournée vers l'exploration de nos abîmes, aimait les garçons, il s'est aussi lié à quelques femmes avec passion. Voici les sept et de ses échappées féminines.

Par SOPHIE MAZAUD et FRÉDÉRIQUE VERLEY,
photographie INEZ VAN, SAPFERRIE et VINOORMATALION,
réalisation EMMANUELLE ALT.

Le lisse noir.

Lancée il y a deux ans par les stylistes de mode, la vague des cheveux raides au rouleau compresseur vire au ras de marée. Mode d'emploi.

Un air de famille.

La mode est au jeu, le luxe, un art de vivre le léger. Célébrée par Oliviero Toscani avec Rocco, son fils, dans le rôle de photographe, et Ali et Lola, les filles corsetées mannequins d'un jour, la grand-messe paillettes de la haute couture devient une fête de famille.

Photographie OLIVIERO TOSCANI
réalisation MARIE AMELIA RAULT

TRANS GENRE

Comment on en être avec un sexe féminin se transforme en homme à l'adolescence. Comment prend souche une famille grecque transplantée sur le sol américain. Comment Jeffrey Eugenides, l'auteur intimiste de "Virgin Suicides", accouche en neuf ans d'un roman épique en forme d'odyssée. Best-seller annoncé. "Middlesex" (éd. de l'Olivier) réserve plus d'une métamorphose à ses lecteurs.

Par PHILIPPE BINET
photographie JEAN WELTERS

UNE CULTURE SE DÉFINIT par ceux qu'a lus. La Nouvelle Zélande...

LÀ-BAS, TOUT AU BOUT DE L'OCÉAN PACIFIQUE, LA NOUVELLE ZÉLANDE, LA-TERRE DU LONG NUAGE - DES MAORIS. CE PAYS, L'UN DES PLUS ISOLÉS DE LA PLANÈTE, SUSCITE AUJOURD'HUI L'ENGOUEMENT DE L'HÉMISPHÈRE NORD, AVEC QUELQUES ARGUMENTS DE POIDS : SES PAYSAGES, LA QUALITÉ DE VIE ET LE DYNAMISME D'UN MELTING-POT CULTUREL MARQUÉ PAR LA VITALITÉ DE LA COMMUNAUTÉ MAORIE. VOYAGE ET RENCONTRES.

Par SIMONE ELLIS.

GUIDE PRATIQUE

La couleur du désir

Photographie ALBERTO TESTINO
réalisation CAROLINE WOLTELEK

Peau D'ange

SAM HASKINS A TOUJOURS RACONTÉ DES HISTOIRES. DEPUIS LES ANNÉES 60, DEPUIS COWBOY KATE OU NOVEMBER GIRL - DEUX DE SES LIVRES D'IMAGES - SES MISES EN SCÈNE FLUIDES SONT DES EXPÉDITIONS POÉTIQUES À LA RECHERCHE DE LA BEAUTÉ NUE.

PHOTOGRAPHE AMOUREUX DU FOND ET DE LA FORME, SA SENSIBILITÉ DÉLICATE ET SÛRE AGIT COMME UN ENCHANTEMENT.

Photographie SAM HASKINS
réalisation EMMANUELLE ALT

Mortelles pâleurs.

LES FEMMES FATALES S'EMPOISONNENT POUR ATTEINDRE LA BLANCHEUR IDÉALE. APRÈS UN SIÈCLE D'ADORATION DU SOLEIL, LA COSMÉTIQUE RETROUVE LE GOÛT DU TEINT DE LIS, DE VÉNÉNEUX AU NATUREL, À LA RECHERCHE DU TEINT PARFAIT.
Par LIZ GOLDWYN et STÉPHANIE DAUPHINOIS.
Illustration LAURIE PAULE.

Qui êtes-vous Ralph Lauren?

Par JACQUES BRUNEL

RALPH LAUREN, LE CAÏD DU CHIC RELAX MADE IN USA, FÊTE LES TRENTE-CINQ ANS DE SON LABEL. L'OCCASION DE DÉVOILER LA DUALITÉ TROUBLANTE DU WINNER AUX YEUX DE GLACE. UNE NATURE DE COW-BOY, DANDY DANS LA DOUBLURE.

Carte postale.

Photographe DABRI PICCININOTTI, réalisation CLAIRE DHELENS.

Peace & Rock à New York

Par SERGE POUVREAU, photographe DAVID ARMSTRONG.

OUI, LA VIE PEUT ÊTRE DOUCE À NEW YORK. WILLIAMSBURG, EXTENSION NORD DE BROOKLYN, RESSEMBLE À UNE BOURGADE DE PROVINCE MAIS VIBRE COMME UN GHETTO MODE. ET LA JAILLISSENT AUSSI LES NOUVELLES FLEURS DU ROCK'N ROLL.

Marceau,
LA VÉRITÉ

TÉCHINÉ
LE
MAG NIFIQUE

Rendez-vous.

95 C.

Volupté fétiche, plastique aux reliefs émouvants et lèvres incendie érotiques **une mode au plus près du corps** et célèbrent la tentation d'atouts très chair.

possession.

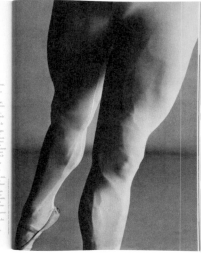

pretty woman.

La cuissarde est un choix propice au vertige. Ajouté en haut des cuisses, accentué par l'impact d'une mini, l'accessoire clé de la saison est un coup de fouet sur l'allure et sur le nerf du désir.

Ego girl.

Splash!

La parade sur le sable d'une plastique de championne avec déflagration de couleurs, mélange d'hiver et d'été avec fourrure par 40° à l'ombre, transforme le rituel du bain de soleil en une transe mode incandescente.

jungle forever.

La chair du diamant.

Par ANNA ROZEN

«Un diamant, c'est beaucoup d'argent et beaucoup de poésie», disait une jeune femme très passionnée. Pourtant, les envies et les traitements de cet objet de désir paraissent en train de changer, constate la journaliste Sophie Delavie. Pour ce qui est de la poésie et du fantasme, leur éclat est infini comme en témoigne la nouvelle inédite de la romancière Anna Rozen.

MAGISTRAL, DANS LA QUAI FOULETTE MES SEMBLABLES ENCHAÎNÉS...

...Bons baisers de Russie

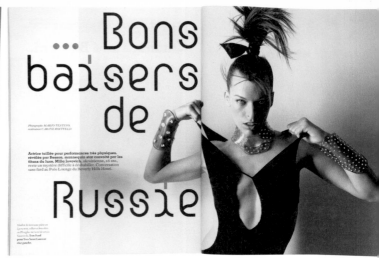

Photographie MARIO TESTINO, réalisation CARINE ROITFELD

Actrice taillée pour performances très physiques, révélée par Besson, mannequin star convoité par les titans du luxe, Milla Jovovich, ukrainienne, 26 ans, reste un mystère difficile à déshabiller. Conversation sans fard au Polo Lounge du Beverly Hills Hotel.

Pour avoir l'énergie et les formes de Milla, deux coachs expliquent leur technique: travailler les muscles en longueur pour étoffer le haut du corps.

Par ASTRID TAUPIN

Brigitte de Villebonne, coach au Waou

Martine Curtis-Oakes, prof de Pilates

Shopping fermeté

New York dolls

Long ISLAND BABY

Absolument fabuleuse.

Gueule d'ange.

MATISSE PICASSO, frères en passion.

QUELQUES MIETTES AU FOND DU LIT

*Par FRANÇOIS-MARIE NETTI,
photographie ERWAN FROTIN*

IL Y A DES INSTANTS QUI MÉRITENT UNE DROLE EXCLUSIVITÉ. JUSTE QUATRE MURS, LES VÔTRES. ENFIN CEUX DE VOTRE CHAMBRE. D'HÔTEL DE PRÉFÉRENCE. LA VIE COMME LA NOTE ONT ALORS UNE PETITE TOUCHE TERRIBLEMENT SALÉE.

LE ROOM-SERVICE...

Pour ne pas perdre le petit garçon simple en moi garçon simple en moi, Messieurs

Noël Gisele au soleil,

*Photographie MARIO TESTINO,
réalisation CARINE ROITFELD.*

INSTANTANÉS D'HIER ET POSES D'AUJOURD'HUI. ALBUM DE FAMILLE OU PAPIER GLACÉ : LE NATUREL ÉCLATANT DE GISELE, PETITE FILLE CHOYÉE DEVENUE LE FÉMININ ABSOLU. EST LE SOLEIL SUR LA PHOTO. CONFIDENCES D'UN TOP SACRÉ. *Propos recueillis par MARIE PRINTEMPS.*

Passe-temps.

Photographie ERWAN FROTIN, réalisation LUDIVINE POIBLANC.

*Photographie THOMAS SCHENK,
réalisation CLAUDIA POIBLANC.*

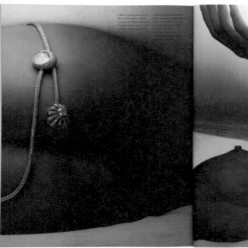

*Photographie MARIO TESTINO,
réalisation CARINE ROITFELD.*

Margherita bella

LA GÉNÉROSITÉ DE SOPHIA, LA FRAÎCHEUR DE CLAUDIA, L'ÉCLAT DE GINA... MADEMOISELLE MISSONI EST L'HÉRITIÈRE DE LA BEAUTÉ SOLAIRE, SENSUELLE ET PUDIQUE, DES HÉROÏNES DU CINÉMA ITALIEN. BELLISSIMA, TROISIÈME GÉNÉRATION : ELLE EST LA PETITE-FILLE DE LA DOLCE VITA.

*Coiffure Alain Pichon, Mise en beauté Charlotte Tilbury,
Maquillage Estée Lauder, Manucure Lorraine Griffin.*

Jessica Embrasse-moi!

*Photographie TERRY RICHARDSON,
réalisation EMMANUELLE ALT.*

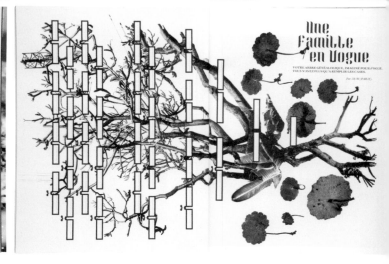

Une famille en Vogue

VOTRE ARBRE GÉNÉALOGIQUE, IMAGINÉ POUR VOGUE, VOUS N'AVEZ PLUS QU'À REMPLIR LES CASES.
Par JEAN PARIS.

Par OLIVIER ZAHM

Les guépards

D&G & GABBANA BRÛLE COMME LE SEL DE LA MÉDITERRANÉE. DUO MÂLE CORSÉ. DOMENICO DOLCE ET STEFANO GABBANA RÊVENT D'UNE FEMME ENTRE LA MAMMA ET LA PUTAIN. À LA TÊTE D'UN EMPIRE EN CROISSANCE, SACRÉ ELDORADO DES BÊTES DE MODE, LE TANDEM DU «SEXE, D'UN EMPIRE PARTAGE TOUT, LA GLOIRE ET LA VIE PRIVÉE.

Je me souviens de Louise

Par HÉLÈNE ALANE

Helena devant sa maison de vacances au Danemark.

Dans les bras d'Helena

Par S.W. MEYLENKA photographie MARIO TESTINO

DIFFICILE D'ATTEINDRE CET IDÉAL DE PERFECTION. THE LOOK, LE REGARD, COMME BACALL. LES PETITS OS DE CHAT, COMME KATE MOSS. LA LONGUEUR DE SPECTACULAIRE D'UNE MISS UNIVERS. HELENA CHRISTENSEN, 34, TOP-MODEL, STAR DES ANNÉES 90, PASSÉE DU CADRE DES PHOTOGRAPHES VEDETTES À SON PROPRE OBJECTIF.

Vacances anglaises.

Par BERND ET TINA FORM, photographie MARC-CLAUDE MARTIN

DAMIAN HIRST EST LE CRÉATEUR QUE LES COLLECTIONNEURS S'ARRACHENT, ET LE PERSONNAGE QUE LE PUBLIC ANGLAIS ADORE HAÏR. IL, 42 ANS, UNE FAMILLE HEUREUSE ET DES AMIS PARFAITS. IL EST UN GRAND ARTISTE, MÊME PENDANT LES VACANCES.

Réveillon à la Tour d'Ivoire

Par FRANÇOIS-MARIE SZÜTY, photographe ERWAN FROTIN

L'INSTANT FATAL. CHAQUE ANNÉE, ON A L'IMPRESSION DE L'AVOIR SUFFISAMMENT CÉLÉBRÉ. POUR L'OUBLIER. TÊTU, IL REVIENT AVEC SON ÉTERNELLE TÊTE DE CACHET D'ASPIRINE. SES SERPENTINS ET SES TÉMÉRITÉS SOUS LE COUP. CETTE ANNÉE, TENDEZ-LUI UN PIÈGE. UN RENDEZ-VOUS OÙ VOUS N'APPARAÎTREZ PAS.

PRESCRIPTION DE NOËL

Bambina.

TOUTE PETITE, MARGHERITA GAMBARAÏT DANS LES BACKSTAGES MISEGNI COMME ON JOUA À CACHE-CACHE DANS LES GRENIERS D'UNE MAISON DE FAMILLE. ELLE A PRESQUE 20 ANS, ELLE ÉTUDIE LA PHILOSOPHIE, ET POSE POUR VOGUE. ELLE NOUS OUVRE SON ALBUM DE SOUVENIRS.

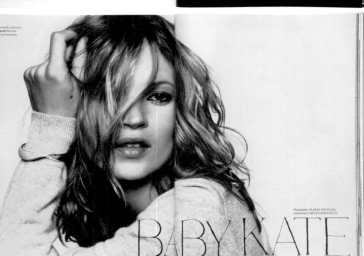

BABY KATE

Photographie MARIO TESTINO, réalisation ORANE POETMZ

Il paraît que Kate Moss rêve de cinéma. Pour l'heure, la brindille, élue top 97, pique au milieu des années 90, comme peut ses orages intimes, joue le rôle de maman. L'écrivain Marc Lambron, séduit par cette femme-enfant d'l'insolence décalée et fatale, lui verrait bien un grand écran. En héroïne du siècle, mi-rock mi-pop. Toujours classe.

Par MARC LAMBRON

Cuir ultra-violet. Perfecto argent, leggings irisés, mini-robe incendiaire claquent sur la peau humide d'un corps sous tension et activent une mode tonique et sensual chic inspirée du film *Flashdance*.

ON AIR

L'art de vivre sur la paille.

I ♥ JOANA

HAWAIIAN PUNCH

Calvin Klein, éros malgré lui.

Garçons en ville.

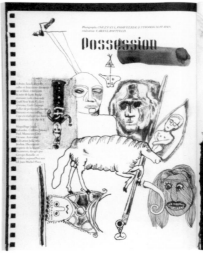

Possession

Patrick Kelly: respect.

Par LIZ GOLDWYN

EN MOINS DE CINQ ANS, AVEC POUR SEULES ARMES L'IRONIE, L'AUTODÉRISION ET L'ÉMOTION, PATRICK KELLY A SU TRANSFORMER LES PRÉJUGÉS RACIAUX EN FÉTICHES DE MODE. AUTANT QU'EN OBJETS DE SUBVERSION. DU MISSISSIPPI À PARIS, LE DESTIN DE MÉTÉORE BLACK DE LA MODE DES ANNÉES 80.

Les trésors de John.

Par FARID CHENOUNE, photographie DOUGLAS DE RYS

C'est la première
séance photo d'Anna
sous l'œil ému de sa mère,
Pat Cleveland,
icône des seventies glamour.
À 14 ans, une mode XXI, pour jouer aux grandes.
Mais sans maquiller le charme adolescent.

anna

Photographes
INEZ VAN LAMSWEERDE
& VINOODH MATADIN,
réalisation
EMMANUELLE ALT.

Scoop : l'allure est tonique, le corps plein d'esprit,
le moral au beau fixe. Plongez en apnée dans une dynamique
de championnes dopées grand teint au graphisme 80
et aux motifs bucoliques.

ROUGE!

Photographie GUSTAVO TOSCANO, réalisation MARIE-AMÉLIE LEROY.

Haute tension.

L'énergie mini-mini, poussée aux puissance maximale, pour un style électrochoc, tout en fétiches et en couleur. Une mode d'expressions en XXS.

Par VINCENT JAVET
photographie MARTIEN MULDER

Harry l'auteur.

Un monument en Hollande, célèbre aux États-Unis et en Allemagne, souvent cité pour le prix Nobel. Harry Mulisch est l'invité vedette du salon du livre, cette année consacré aux Pays-Bas. Ou vit l'humour, interrogé ce jeune homme vert de 75 ans. Réponse dans son œuvre, l'une des plus brillantes du XXe siècle.

stop ou encore?

Une journée avec Rose Marie

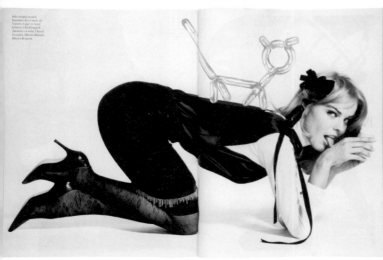

Course eu sac

Parka en gabardine de laine à capuche imperméable.
Gouttières gemellés en nylon.
Mocassin à semelle Go1roud. Polo en coton tigré.
Sur-chemise et sur-vêtement fausse Polka Fent.

Pantalon de jogging en Nylon. Solej Naturaliste. Gouttière en laine et cuire manteau en piqué de coton. Laines Gerhard. Polo en coton tigré. Sac en simili-cuir vernis extensible à semelle revêtue en plongée lapel. Balenciaga.

Photographe DAVID SIMS,
réalisatrice MARIE-AMÉLIE SAUVÉ.

Sport études

Coiffeur Sandy. Maquillage Jakob Kokobou. Mannequin Mariam Bouroon. Assistante réalisation Katrien Jacobs.

QU'EST-CE QU'UN «C» ARTISTE AUJOURD'HUI?

Par MARTIN BETHENOD, portrait PHILIPPE CHANCEL.

Parc Central.

INVITÉE À LA DOCUMENTA DE KASSEL, EN ALLEMAGNE, GRAND-MESSE INTERNATIONALE DE L'ART CONTEMPORAIN, DOMINIQUE GONZALEZ-FOERSTER A CRÉÉ UN PARC UNIVERSEL, UNIQUE, LITTÉRAIRE ET CINÉMATOGRAPHIQUE. BLOW-UP SUR L'UNE DES ARTISTES FRANÇAISES LES PLUS RECHERCHÉES DU MOMENT.

Par SYLVIE LILANNE, photographe CRAIG McDEAN.

ELEGANT MAN
Mauvais garçon

LE PLUS BEAU DÉFILÉ 2002, C'ÉTAIT LUI, ALEXANDER McQUEEN, LE VILAIN GARÇON DES FAUBOURGS DE LONDRES, EST UNE ÉTOILE SOUS L'AILE DU TITANESQUE GUCCI GROUP. FIDÈLE À SES DEMONS.

Baignade interdite (depuis 1975).

Par EMMANUEL BURDE Jr, illustration ARCHIVIAUM.

PRESQUE TRENTE ANS APRÈS, *JAWS / LES DENTS DE LA MER*, LE FILM QUI REMPLIT LES SALLES ET VIDE LES PLAGES, N'A RIEN PERDU DE SON MORDANT. N'Y PENSEZ VOUS JAMAIS EN ENTRANT DANS L'EAU? DÉCRYPTAGE D'UN MYTHE MODERNE ET DE SES SÉQUELLES.

Werner, un chic type.

Des millions gagnés, quelques ans... Werner Schreyer, le mâle modèle du moment... Une vie de glamour et de chaos... great star.
Par MARIE-PANT PERRA.

La poupée.

On y lon des plus charmants instincts de l'enfance féminine incarné par le sublime Loettito Costu, version haute couture, dont les poses de danseuse et le teint de rose transcendent les plus beaux specimens Celluloid.

Photographe GLEN LUCHFORD,
réalisatrice ANASTASIA BARRERI.

アーティストとしての作法が
雑誌デザインに新しい風を吹き込む

　仕事場を見れば、その人がどんなタイプのアートディレクターなのかがわかる。この人はビジネスマン寄りだな、この人はアーティスト寄りだな、などなど。画家のアトリエのような雰囲気。M/M（Paris）のオフィスを訪れて、ボクは自分の予想が当たっていたのを実感した。彼らの活動を見ていて、常々アーティストに片足を突っ込んでいるようだと思っていたからだ。彼らが『VOGUE PARIS』を手掛けたのが2002年からの2年間。それから数年後、彼らはアーティストとしての評価をずいぶん高めている。

デザイナーとアーティスト

　「活動を始めた頃から、自分たちの存在について、デザイナーであると同時にアーティストであると捉えていました。その姿勢が最近になってアートの世界でも認められてきたのだと思います」正直に告白すると、初めて彼らが担当した『VOGUE PARIS』を見たとき、その仕事に対するボクの評価は高くなかった。もちろん当時から、デザイン方法の斬新さや今まで誰もやっていないことにチャレンジする気概は見て取れたが、雑誌デザインという観点から見ると、やや雑な面も感じていた。今振り返ってみると、その頃からアーティストとしての地位を確立していく兆しがあったのかもしれない。

　「あの2年間は、僕たちにとって、とても強烈な経験でした。担当することが決まった後、すぐに雑誌全体のデザインを見直すことから始め、内容の再構築、メッセージの再定義、ヴィジュアルランゲージの作り直しなどに6ヶ月を要しました。それら全ての要素が仕上がった後に、最終的なデザインをスムーズに変化させていったんです。デザインはクラシックなイメージで、かつ私たちのよい部分を生かした形に仕上げました。具体的なデザインの作業は短期間で行い、その間に『VOGUE PARIS』をファッション業界の人気俳優のような存在へと変身させたんです。もち

なって雑誌を作るとしたら、どのような雑誌を作り上げるのだろうか。

「『VOGUE PARIS』の仕事を辞めてから、『i-D』、『Purple Fashion』、『V magazine』、『W magazine』などの多くのファッション雑誌からオファーを受けました。通常、ADを選ぶときはその出版社に関わりのある人を選ぶものですが、彼らは『VOGUE PARIS』とは別の出版社にも関わらず僕たちを必要としてくれたんです。

そんなふうに、僕たちは雑誌を通してさまざまな題材に関わってきました。『Les Inrockuptible』ではロックカルチャー、『eDEN』ではハウスミュージックやクラブミュージック、『Documents sur l'art』、『Frog』ではコンテンポラリーアート、『Wow』ではナイトクラブカルチャー、『VOGUE PARIS』ではファッション……といった具合に。これからさらに、クリエイティブディレクターとして『Arena Homme Plus』を手掛けることが決まっています。今のところ自分たちの仕事に満足していますね」

さまざまな雑誌を経験した2人が作り上げる『Arena Homme Plus』。今度はマガジンデザインの作法にのっとるのか、または彼らのアートを雑誌に落とし込むのか。ただ、間違いなく新しいデザインスタイルを見せてくれるのだとワクワクする。

『Arena Homme Plus』のその先

「もしこれから先、雑誌を手掛けることがあるなら、時代性にとらわれず、ある種、勢いを失ったような雑誌に面白みを感じますね。そういった雑誌は、広告キャンペーンの対象としてのみ成立している場合が多く、見向きもしない人もいるはずです。そういった雑誌を興味深いものに作り変えていくことは、面白いチャレンジだと思うので」

『VOGUE PARIS』、『Arena Homme Plus』を経たその先も、彼らはマガジンデザインの世界に新しい風を吹き込み続けるのだろう。東京とパリ、約1万キロも離れているけど、彼らの雑誌デザインに対する姿勢を見ていると、ボクは何らかの親近感を感じてしまう。

ろん、かなりのプレッシャーはありましたけどね」

M/M (Paris) が作る雑誌

その後、『i-D』『V magazine』などの雑誌で、ゲストADとして招かれているM/M(Paris)の2人。もし自分たちが編集長と

M/M (Paris)

Founded in 1992. Michael Amzalag and Mathias Augustyniak is the graphic design and creative duo. Michael Amzalag studied at the Ecole Nationale Superieure des Arts Decoratifs, Paris and Mathias Augustyniak studied at the Royal College of Arts, London. They have forged longstanding collaborations with musician as Bjork, Madonna and etc, artists as Pierre Huyghe, Liam Gillick and etc, fashion brands as Yohji Yamamoto, Jill Sander and etc. M/M have held many exhibitions at Gallery Rocket (Tokyo/2003&2004), Palais de Tokyo (Paris/2005), Centre Pompidou (Paris/2005), etc.

エム / エム (パリス)

ミカエル・アムザラムとマティアス・オグスティニアックにより1992年にパリで結成されたグラフィックデザイン・アートディレクターデュオ。アムザラムは1990年にパリの国立装飾美術学校（ENSAD）を卒業。一方、オグスティニアックは1991年にロンドンのロイヤルカレッジオブアートのグラフィックデザイン＆アートディレクション修士課程を修了。ビョークやマドンナなどのミュージシャン、ピエール・ユイグやリアム・ギリックなどのアーティスト、ヨウジヤマモトやジルサンダーなどのファッションブランド他、ジャンルを超えたさまざまなコラボレーションを行う。Gallery Rocket(東京 /2003 & 2004)、Palais de Tokyo（パリ /2005）、Centre Pompidou（パリ /2005）などエキジビションも多数。

横尾忠則

TADANORI YOKOO

(流行通信, 流行通信OTOKO)

Ryuko Tsushin   Ryuko Tsushin-OTOKO

What I did at *Ryuko Tsushin* was to take the stuff of magazine design, and figure out how to do away with design

The *Ryuko Tsushin* of which Tadanori Yokoo was art director had a remarkable presence. There is a species of graphic design that only the singular Tadanori Yokoo can get away with. Even if at times it was difficult to read, even if it failed to convey the information, one could always expect an encounter with the transcendent power of art. Part of the magazine's appeal was the thrill of knowing the potential of all magazines.

— Since you put out *Ryuko Tsushin*, many more people have openly declared that magazines should be designed freely: another sense in which the magazine achieved so much. I'm hoping today to explore the origin of that originality.

"A magazine starts with a theme for each page: the question of what each page is trying to do. That's what interested me: the idea of choosing the design needed to present a single idea. First I was approached by Hanae Mori and given the position of art director. My personal aim was to give the magazine itself a bit more life. Although well beyond my authority, I often made my views known regarding the editorial content as well. I really did do all sorts of things, now that I think about it. Like making all the pages apart from the advertising black and white. I also proposed turning just the ads upside down, although that idea never came to fruition. However it seems the more we experimented like that, and the more daringly we flouted the conventions of magazine design, the more copies we sold. So Mori-san asked me to stay on, but I didn't fancy the pressure, so committed initially to just a year. For my last issue I actually took the photos myself, using a variety of cameras to capture back views of women's hair for a spread over several pages. I then worked on the men's magazine *Ryuko Tsushin OTOKO* for a while, where I did things like place singer and actor Akihiro Miwa on the cover against a gold background."

Magazine design with a poster sensibility

— So you had a lot of freedom. It all looks very new and fresh even now.

"Around that time Kohei Sugiura was doing some excellent work, and the trend was tight letter-spacing. So I suggested taking the opposite tack and opening up space between characters in all the titles, main text etc. The posters I'd done up to then had been generously spaced, and it gives the pages a really loose look. Which for me was a new sensation. Although these days spacing like that is standard practice in the advertising world, so it's no longer especially interesting or humorous. It's like there are fragments of the old *Ryuko Tsushin* around the place. I do seem to have been ahead of the times in terms of what you might call 'visual vision', but wasn't especially trying to be futuristic; just doing what I felt like at the time. It's no fun using something somebody else has come up with, so I thought I'd try something different, even if it wasn't that good."

— Legend has it that you did all the mechanicals, a job usually performed by the technicians. Is this true?

"It is. Why not – I love it. It'd be a shame to let the technicians have all the fun. Plus I'd never done magazine design before. I'd bound books, but was pretty much an amateur when it came to magazines. So I didn't know how they were assembled, and was producing each spread as if making a poster.

Even so I was very conscious of the sequence of the pages, for example making them flow in a cinematic sort of way. When people enter a movie theater, there's that initial period where they sit down, and adjust their posture in the seat. So I threw in something to make an impact right at that point. I thought about the overall narrative of the magazine in ways like that. But because with magazines the copy turns up at all different times, you can't assemble the thing in order. So it was like working on film rushes. I deliberately incorporated inconsistencies, a lack of coherence. A lack of responsibility actually, is a vital part of the mix, believe it or not. Fortunately my design partners in crime Teruhiko Yumura and Shoichi Yabu were quite irresponsible in their own way. Meaning they were free-thinking and flexible. If people can't have a bit of fun, I find it very hard to work with them (laughs)."

Figuring out how to do away with design

— Back then I was designing a magazine called *Taiyo*, and your work seemed incredibly fresh to me.

"I'm delighted you felt that way, but it really didn't go down well with people my own age and older. Don't you think the design of *Ryuko Tsushin* was a bit staid before I came along? It was well put together, but said nothing about the soul of those who produced it. I suspect that at the time, people thought that because it was a magazine, such things shouldn't be visible. That was the theory of magazine layout, and it was academic in the extreme. The ADC (Art Directors Club) jury had also become part of the Establishment, and were very conservative. The moment they spotted something even remotely new, they were on guard. So Teruhiko and Shoichi also used to bemoan their lack of credit from the ADC. Back then, art and design were still rivals. This is 1981, remember. Just at the time I was switching to art. Switching from graphic design to painting is in a sense the task of doing away with design. In short, what I did at *Ryuko Tsushin* was to take the stuff of magazine design, and figure out how to discard design. But if discarding was that simple, you'd end up with rubbish, so I had Shoichi and co., who were usually doing the editorial, direct the traffic as I moved on. Except they were also the types to ignore the lights (laughs). Stop on green and go on red: that's the kind of thing we were trying to create. The editor Hideko Otake also let us do things our way, and took an interest in our various explorations. Rather than trying to throw her weight around, she accepted what we came up with. So it was an excellent environment to work in."

— **Looking back you had quite an impressive lineup of people working on the magazine. How did you work out the feature content, casting and such?**

"The editors would come up with a broad outline for the editorial, then come to my place for a meeting, where we would decide everything from how we were going to do the photos, to the cameraman. For example, use the time from evening through night into sunrise to shoot in one location on a rooftop. Nobody ever complained, even about concepts like that, and they'd all throw themselves into it with great enthusiasm. I would contact the cameramen directly too. I remember calling Nobuyoshi Araki. When I asked if he'd be interested in shooting for a fashion magazine he initially turned me down flat, but eventually I persuaded him to take just one underwear shot, in black and white. Araki and a chemise: the perfect match, don't you think (laughs)? When I tried to get Shinya Fujiwara to shoot a Tokyo fashion show for us, he refused for ages, but I lured him by playing on the theme of his photos, convincing him that there was no point having the Silk Road end at Todaiji; it would be much more typically Silk Road to end behind the scenes at a Tokyo fashion show. In the

end, anything will do. To get these guys on board, you have to use all your powers of persuasion. Creatives are stubborn, clammed up beasts. You have to prize them open. To me that was the director's job, so I even did the negotiating.

Apart from that, when explaining my vision of the photos I wanted a cameraman to take, I often described it in terms of 'that scene in that film' or similar. I never said I wanted pictures 'like so-and-so takes them'. Films, kabuki, novels... With the atmosphere of Hemingway's NOTE etc. Which was OK if they had the same tastes as me, but I bet a few had to rush off and frantically read the book."

— **Creatives love being given an image from a genre that is visually different and working to achieve something close to that. You could say for example, "Shoot it like Richard Avedon" and it would be easy to understand, but maybe a little too simple.**

Striving to shut out influences

— **Have you seen any magazines lately?**
"None at all. I don't look at magazines, read magazines, or touch magazines. When I was younger I was influenced in that way to some degree, but looking back, I wasn't very interested in other people's design or posters. I was interested in film, theater, music, literature and such, genres different to my own. Plus, if you look at magazines you can be influenced by them, and find yourself wanting to copy the techniques. To avoid that, I shut myself off from information as I work. That's still the case.

At the moment I'm doing contemporary art, right? So I shut out all contemporary art. I don't go to exhibitions, I don't look at any books or magazines. If I don't do this, I might be influenced by contemporary art trends, or end up pigeonholed in a particular way. Which isn't very interesting either. I can do things that capture the atmosphere of the times, but that ends up being a single genre. Even if that genre per se becomes the focus of attention, it 's not everlasting. Plus if you fall into that trap, when times change you have to change with them."

Tadanori Yokoo wants to do things no one else has ever done. Because he loathes imitation, he purposely creates an environment free of outside influences. I realized with a jolt that even such a legendary figure does not simply pluck ideas out of the sky, but makes an enormous effort to achieve originality. More than anyone, Yokoo is a true defier of borders who has crossed the barrier from art to magazine design, and back again.

東京

MITSUHIRO MATSUDA
YŌJI YAMAMOTO

REI KAWAKUBO
ISSEY MIYAKE

紅　育

HALSTON
PERRY ELLIS
HOLLY HARP

伯林 1930　BERLIN 1980

紅

BEAUTY

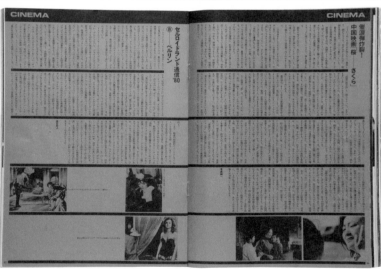

FOOD

茄　子

浪漫的

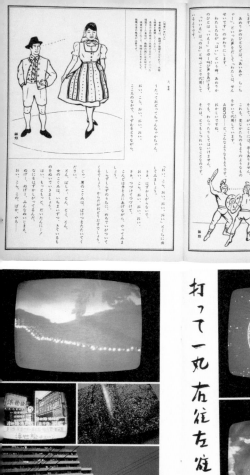

Go On A Stage

CASTA DIVA
spectacle de Maurice Béjart

三宅一生

ファッション・デザイナーのつくる舞台衣裳

モーリス・ベジャール

打って一丸右往左往

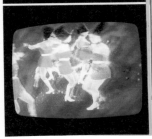

ビューティー

ART

松田光弘

ヨシノヒロコ

ザンドラ・ローズ

稲葉賀恵

山本耀司

CINEMA

CINEMA

YANKS〈ヤンクス〉＊LES CINÉMASTES VARIÉS〈つかこうへい

フェイム 吉見佑子

今 中年 映画

La salade frisée aux lardons

FOOD シェフとの対話 10 サラダ 写真 半田也寸志

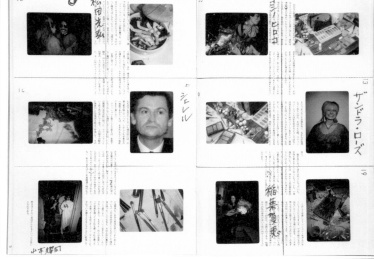

ART 瀬戸内寂聴とダーガンジェロ 写真 有田泰而

BEAUTY

あし

写真　操上和美　モデル　深山エネ

FOOD

フルーツのグラタン

シェフとの対話　14　文　森英恵

写真　操上和美

ARCHITECTURE

建築の失楽園 15　庭または時間　植田実

写真　山田脩二

僕の樹下美人たち—3

カシミール・パキスタン・アフガニスタン

写真・文　若松謙三

SOLAR HOUR

K SAFETY FILM 5017

写真　小暮徹

彩

写真　鋤田正義

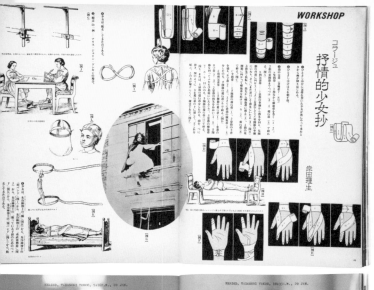

コラージュ

抒情的少女抄

岸田理生

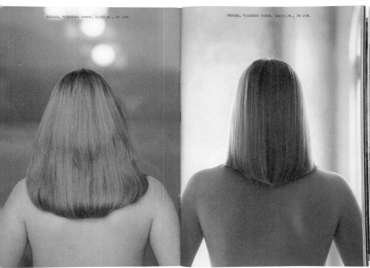

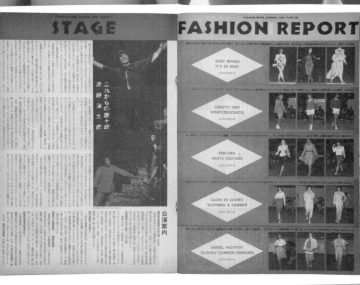

STAGE

FASHION REPORT

これからの唐十郎

津野海太郎

公演案内

ISSEY MIYAKE
IT'S SO HEAT

CERUTTI 1881
SPORT(DESCENTE)

KIMIJIMA
HAUTE COUTURE

CLOVE VS CLOVES
'81SPRING & SUMMER

DANIEL HECHTER
'81EARLY SUMMER (ONWARD)

湯村輝彦とロバート・ベクトル

ART
Focus

photograph by Teruhiko Yumura

KNOC

写真―山田修二　　時間または都市　植田実　　建築の失楽園 16

ARCHITECTURE

MOGA

僕の樹下美人たち 4. インド（ラジャスタン）

写真・文 若杉憲司

Coloring Puzzle on Stage

バレエとアートの共演

写真—鋤田正義

CALIGULA

ペントハウス、品位の限界

「カリギュラ」は歴史映画だ

高橋伴明

FOOD　Photo: Yutaka Takanashi

シェフとの対話 8

兎
LE LAPIN RÔTI

森英恵

ART　Photo: Norito Yoshimura

絵の第一印象
ウェッセルマンと囈嘔の女

よこすか未美

Look at

Portraits of the 70's

SPECIAL STORY

Too Much Decoration

166

食品美容

写真──小暮徹

杉浦冨美子

祐乗坊英昭

写真──畠山志朗

Japan as No.X

紐　育

HALSTON
PERRY ELLIS
HOLLY HARP

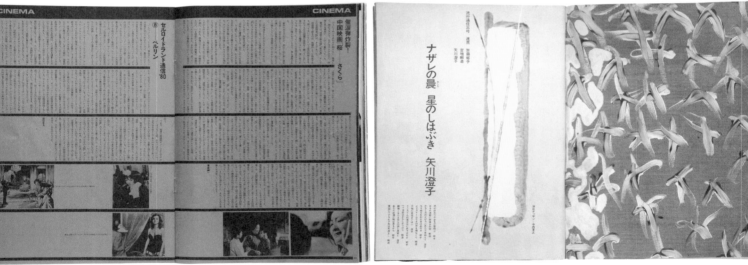

CINEMA

CINEMA

⑧──ベルリン

セルロイドトラム通信'80

催涙弾作製！
中国映画・桜
──さくら──

ナザレの晨　星のしぶき　矢川澄子

ローズ・オレンジ・オークモス・パチュリ・カストレウム

イランイラン・ミルラ・ラベンダー・パディア・カネール

スズラン・ナルシス・ベチベール・シベット・スイカズラ

残像はやがて闇に溶け、仄白い閃きだけが永遠のそして瞬

間の記憶を刻む刃となる。気まぐれ、気ちがい、移り気な

女たち。あえかな香りを無造作に投げ出して、鏡の谷間へ

と墜ちてゆく。絹や真珠や羽根飾りをまとい、揺れる色彩

の炎の中に煌めいて、彼姫の闇から過去と未来を遊び出す。

HALSTON'S SELECTIONS

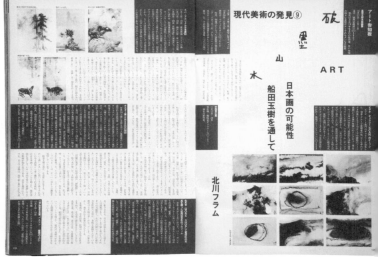

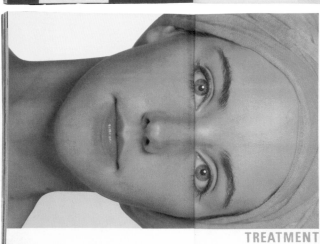

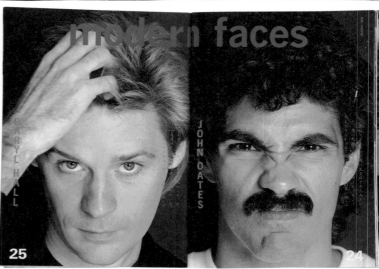

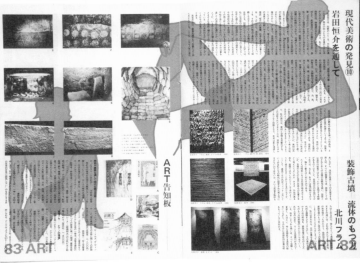

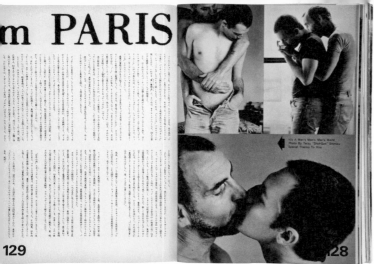

It's A Man's Man's Man's World
Photo By Tetsu "ShotGun" Shimizu
Special Thanks To Hiro

129　128

BACK TO 1981

142　142

147

ちりぬるをわか言はぬ花々　加藤郁子

Model : Roger Black
Cycle wear : Blue Bell

座談会

神聖半カルチュアよ
何処へ行く。

小暮徹　カメラマン
吉見佑子　ライター
西井一夫　ジャーナリスト

バレエを習う
「バラ色のつま先で天国の花園を歩く」
マリー・タリオーニ
市川雅

NUMBER 12

85

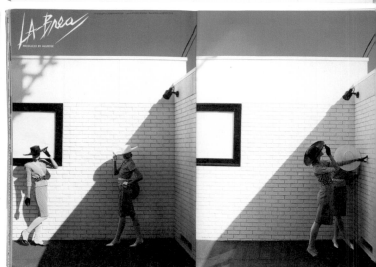

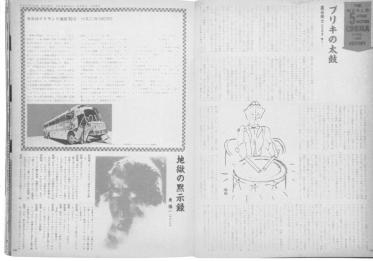

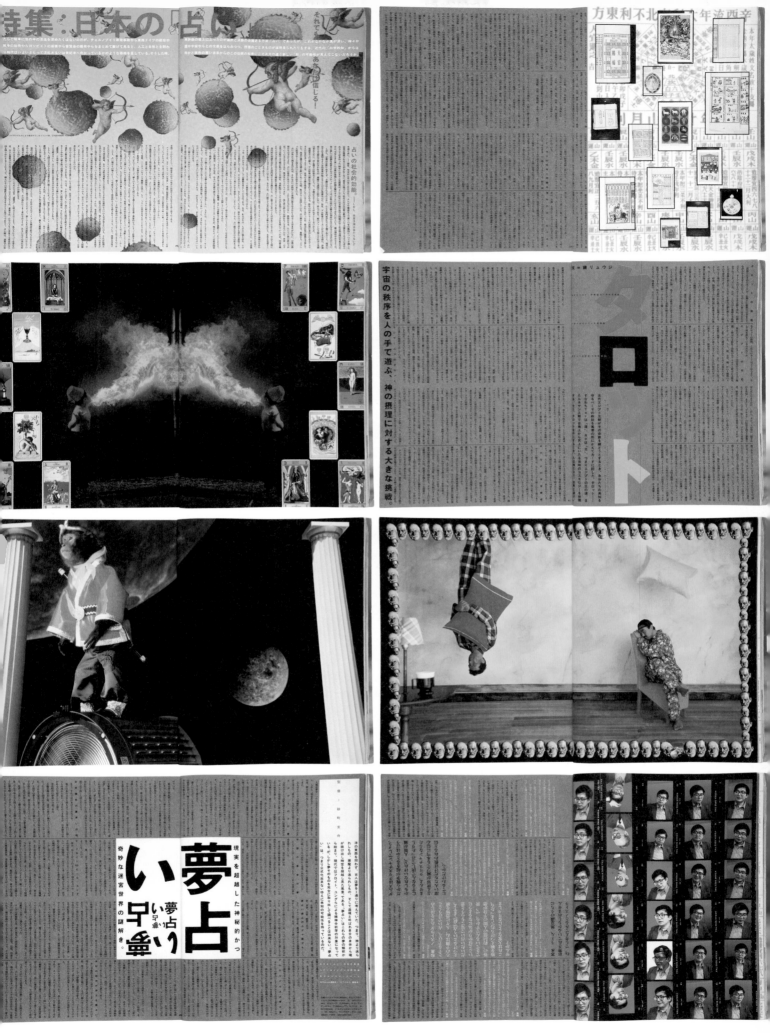

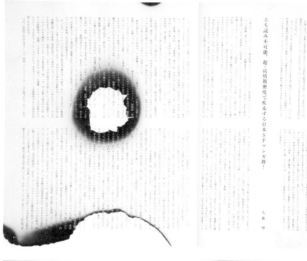

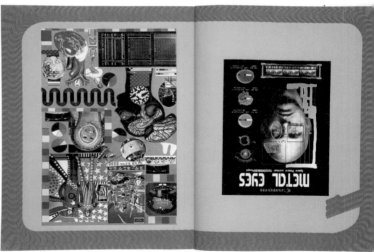

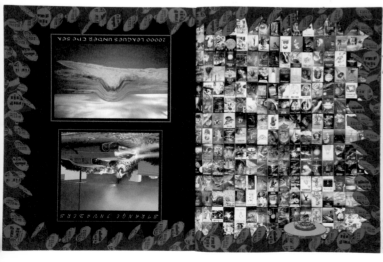

本木雅弘

COVER STORY

僕自身、あるいは国籍な存在

撮影 "横尾忠則"

日本映画における友情の系譜。

加藤泰『瀬戸内少年野球団』から阪本順治『王手』まで。

文・稲村喜彦

人道主義、白樺派の再挑戦。
ネオ白樺派のデジタル感覚を考察する。　文・野沢洋平

女子高生たちの華麗なるブラウン運動。
松苗あけみ、純情クレイジーフルーツを解読する。
文・阿部律子

男と男、男と女、そして女と女、の必要十分条件。
ヨーロッパ上流社会に学んだ友情の条件をミス斎藤が語る。
取材・文 鈴木洋史　写真 神尾良

情報で結ばれた最近の子どもと友情。
ノーライフキングの提案
文 大森望

野田秀樹、演劇を大いに語る。

僕が『流行通信』でやったのは、雑誌デザインの土壌で
いかにデザインを捨てていくかという行為だった

雑誌アートディレクターとして横尾さんが手掛けた『流行通信』は、とても気になる存在だ。"横尾忠則"だから許されるデザインがある。多少読めなくても、情報が伝わらなくても、それを超えるアートの力というものに期待してしまうのだ。それは即ち、雑誌自体の可能性を知る楽しみでもあった。

——横尾さんの『流行通信』が出てから、雑誌のデザインは自由でいいんだと宣言する人が増えました。その意味でも、ものすごく大きな功績のある雑誌だと思うんです。今回は、そのオリジナリティが生まれた原点を探りたいなと。

「雑誌というのはページごとのテーマから始まるでしょ。いったい何をやろうとしているのかっていう思想。そこに興味があったんです。一つの思想を見せるために必要なデザインを選択するという考え方。まず、森英恵さんから依頼があって、アートディレクターという立場を与えられました。僕は、とにかく雑誌自体に生命を与えたいという気持ちでしたね。越権行為ですが、編集内容にまで口出ししたりもしました。本当にいろんなことをしたな。広告以外のページを全部モノクロにしたり、これは実現できなかったけど、広告だけを上下逆さにするっていうのも提案したんですよ。でもそんな試みで、既成の雑誌作りの概念を大胆に破れば破るほど、販売部数は上がってきたらしいんですよね。それで森さんから、もっと続けてほしいって言われたんだけど、それはプレッシャーになるからとりあえず1年間という約束にした。最後の号は僕が写真を撮ったんですよ。女性の髪の後ろ姿を、あらゆる機種のカメラで撮影して、何ページにもわたって載せました。その後しばらくして『流行通信 OTOKO』っていうメンズ誌もやったんだ。金地で美輪明宏さんを表紙にしたりしてね」

ポスターを作る感覚での雑誌デザイン

——そんなに自由にできたんですね。今見てもすごく新しい。

「あの頃は杉浦康平さんがいいお仕事をしていて、字間をつめるのが流行ってたんです。だから僕は逆にタイトルや本文の字間も全部開こうと。それまで作ったポスターでも開いていて、そうするとページがすごく散漫に見えるんですよ。その感じが僕にとっては新しかった。今はもう広告の世界でも開くのが慣例になっちゃって、面白くも可笑しくもないけどね。なんか昔の『流行通信』の断片がそこにあるのかなって。かなりヴィジュアル・ヴィジョンを先読みした感じだけど、特に未来を志向していたわけではなく、そのときの気分でやっていた。他所で確立されているのは面白くないから、とにかく下手でもいいので、変わったものを作ろうと」

——普通は職人さんがする版下作業を、横尾さん自ら行っていたという伝説的な話を聞いたことがあるのですが、本当ですか?

「本当です。特にポスター、装幀にはね。だってそれは楽しいからね。そういう楽しいところを職人さんたちにまかせるのは、もったいないじゃないですか。それと、僕は雑誌デザインって、それまでやったことがなかったんですよ。本の装丁はありましたが、雑誌に関してはほとんど素人。だからやり方がわからなくて、見開きごとにポスターを作るような感覚で作ったわけです。
それでもページの流れはすごく意識してました。映画的にやろうとかね。映画館に入ったとき、お客さんが席に腰掛けて、姿勢を正す間がありますよね。それでここだと思ったところで、バーンとインパクトを与える。そういう全体のストーリーを考えました。だけど雑誌って原稿がバラバラに届くから、順番通りに作れないでしょ。だからラッシュフィルムを作っているような感覚。つじつまが合わないとか、統一感がないということを積極的に取り入れた。無責任っていうのも非常に重要なエレメントなんだよ。幸いデザインを手伝ってくれていた湯村輝彦君や養父正一君も、ある意味、無責任な人たちだったからね。つまり自由ってことね。

遊びのできる人でなきゃ組めないですよ（笑）」

いかにデザインを捨てるかという作業

——ボクは当時『太陽』っていう雑誌のデザインをしてたんですが、横尾さんのデザインをものすごい新鮮に感じました。

「そう言われるとうれしいけど、同世代や上の人たちには本当にウケなかったんだよね。僕がやる前の『流行通信』のデザインって若さがないって思わない？上手にまとめているけど、そこに作家としてのハートが見えてこない。たぶん当時は、雑誌だからそんなものが見えちゃ困るって考え方があったと思うんだよ。それが雑誌のレイアウトセオリーで、非常にアカデミックになってしまっていた。ADCの審査員もエスタブリッシュメントされて、非常に保守的。ちょっと新しいものを見るとガードしちゃうんですよ。だから湯村君も養父君も取り上げてくれないと文句言ってました。つまりあの時代は、まだアート的なものはデザインと対立していたからね。そのときって81年でしょ。そうすると僕がちょうど美術の方に転向した時期なんですよ。デザインから絵に転向するということは、一方でデザインを捨てる作業ですから。つまり『流行通信』でやったことは、デザインという土壌の中で、いかにデザインを捨てていくかということだったと思います。でも、それだけだったらゴミみたいなものになっちゃうから、普段エディトリアルでやっている養父君らに交通整理をしてもらいながら。でも彼らも信号無視するタイプだったからな（笑）。青だから止まって赤だから進めっていうさ、そんなものを作ろうとしていたんだよね。編集長の大竹秀子さんも、僕たちが好き勝手やっているのに寛容で、面白がってくれてましたね。彼女は変に我を通したりしないで、受け入れてくれた。環境がよかったね」

——今見ると豪華なメンバーが関わっていますね。企画内容やキャスティングはどうされていたんですか？

「編集者が編集内容の骨子を決めて、その後、僕の家に来て打合せをしてましたね。そこで撮影方法からカメラマンまで全部決めて。例えば、夕方から夜になり朝日が昇るまでの時間を利用して、1ヶ所の屋上で撮影するとか。そんなコンセプトでも誰も嫌だって言わず、面白がってやってくれていた。カメラマンなんかも僕が直接オファーしたりね。荒木経惟にも僕が電話したな。『ファッション誌に興味ある？』って聞いても『ゼンゼーン』なんて言ってたけど、説得して、下着をモノクロで1枚だけ撮ることになった。荒木にシミーズっていうのがよく似合うでしょ（笑）。東京のファッションショーを藤原新也に撮ってもらおうとしたときも、ずっと断られていたんだけど、彼の撮影テーマに無理やりこじつけて『シルクロードが東大寺で終わるなんてつま

らないよ。東京のファッションショーの楽屋で終わらせた方が、よっぽどシルクロードだ』ってこじつけて納得させたり。結局、何でもいいんですよ。彼らと仕事するには、口八丁手八丁でいかないとダメだもん。クリエイターは頑固だから貝みたいに閉ざしてる。それをガッと開かなきゃいけない。それがディレクターの仕事だと思っていたから、交渉までやりましたよ。
あと僕は撮影してもらいたい写真のイメージを説明するとき、例えば、あの映画の、あのシーンの感じをやりたいんだよねってカメラマンに話すことが多かったかな。誰かが撮った写真のように撮ってほしいとは、一切言わなかった。映画や歌舞伎や小説……。ヘミングウェイの『路地』の雰囲気とかね。向こうも同じ趣味だったらいいんだけど、慌てて本を読まなくちゃいけないなんてこともあっただろうね」

——ヴィジュアルとして違うジャンルのイメージを伝えられて、それにすり寄せていく作業は、クリエイターにとってもやり甲斐がありますよね。例えば「リチャード・アベドンみたいに撮って」と言われたらわかりやすいけど、それって安易すぎてカメラマンに失礼でしょう。

影響をシャットアウトする努力

——横尾さん、最近、雑誌を見ていますか？

「もう全然。雑誌は見ない、読まない、触らないかな。僕も若い頃はそういうものから影響を受けたりしてたけど、振り返ってみると、他人のデザインやポスターにはあまり興味がなかったな。映画や演劇、音楽、文学など、自分とは違うジャンルに関心があった。あと、見ると影響を受けるってこともあるし、手法を真似したくなるってこともあるでしょ。それを避けるために、情報を遮断しながらやる。今でもそうですよ。

今、僕は現代美術をやっているでしょ。だから現代美術は全部シャットアウト。展覧会も行かないし、雑誌も本も全然見ない。そうしないと現代美術にも流行があって、影響を受けたり、その範疇に入ってしまったりする。それだと面白くないしね。時代の空気を掴んだものはできるけれど、それで1つのジャンルになってしまう。そのジャンル自体がクローズアップされることはあっても、永久不滅じゃない。そこにはまると、時代が変わるとまた変わらなきゃいけないしね。常に状況の逆行だね」

誰もやったことがないことをしたい、というスタンス。真似は嫌だから影響されない環境を作る、という話。神様でもアイデアは天から降ってくるのではなく、オリジナリティを出すための努力をしているんだって事実に心を揺さぶられた。横尾さんこそ、アート界から雑誌デザインの塀を乗り越えてやってきた越境者なのだ。

Tadanori Yokoo

Artist. Born 1936 in Hyogo Prefecture. Following a solo show at the Museum of Modern Art in New York, Yokoo's international activities went on to include participation in the Paris, Venice and São Paulo Biennials, and in recent years a string of solo exhibitions at museums including the Museum of Contemporary Art Tokyo; National Museum of Modern Art, Kyoto; and Fondation Cartier pour l'art contemporain in 2006, receiving critical acclaim. He was elected to the Hall of Fame, New York ADC in 2000, received the Purple Ribbon Medal of Honor in 2001, and the Japan Culture Design Award in 2006. His work appears in the permanent collections of MoMA, the Boston Museum of Fine Arts and more than 100 other museums.

横尾忠則

1936年兵庫県生まれ。美術家。1972年にニューヨーク近代美術館で個展。その後もパリ、ベネチア、サンパウロの各ビエンナーレに出品するなど国際的に活躍、近年は東京都近代美術館、京都国立近代美術館など個展を相次いで開催。2006年にはパリのカルティエ現代美術財団で個展を開催し高い評価を得た。2000年ニューヨークアートディレクターズクラブ殿堂入り、2001年紫綬褒章受章、2006年日本文化デザイン大賞受賞。作品はニューヨーク近代美術館、ボストン美術館をはじめ国内外100以上の主要美術館に収蔵されている。http://www.tadanoriyokoo.com/

WORK IN PROGRESS

(SELF SERVICE)

An innovative creative agency develops an alternative magazine

SELF SERVICE magazine has made its mark as one of the most influential fashion and culture magazines of the past decade, while remaining a thoroughly independent force. The magazine is the brainchild of Paris-based creative agency Work in Progress, founded by partners Ezra Petronio and Suzanne Koller. Ezra, who combines creativity with an entrepreneurial spirit, and Suzanne, the inventive source behind much of their work, complement one another perfectly. The pair have built an impressive list of high-profile clients including Comme des Garçons Parfums, Prada, Miu Miu, and Chloé. Whereas the agency comprises the majority of the partners' time, the

magazine remains a highly personal and artistic labor of love.

Building a medium to challenge conservative Paris

Koller and Petronio have recently expanded their offices in the Marais. The first thing one notices upon entering is a wall of bookshelves housing a huge collection of magazines and art books, next to beautifully displayed packaging for the Comme des Garçons and Prada perfumes, which Work in Progress designed. The decor has a minimalist feel, epitomized by the partners' desks, which hold nothing more than their computers, phones, and a perfumed candle. It has been 12 years since Work in Progress founded *SELF SERVICE* magazine. We spoke to Ezra, the magazine's creative director:

SELF SERVICE was launched in 1995, two years after we founded the design agency Work in Progress. It was a very conservative time for art, fashion, and creative expression in Paris. While the city had youth, energy, and creativity in abundance, there was a great divide between the older, mainstream establishment and the alternative, and no medium was documenting all this new talent. This was before Colette, Internet or email. So we launched *SELF SERVICE* to represent this exploding creative energy and to give representation to our generation in the media. We attempted to document the creative world we lived in, featuring such up-and-coming talents as Viktor & Rolf, Raf Simons, or Daft Punk. This was also when the French house music scene was kicking off. In these past 12 years, you could say we've grown with the magazine, which could also be described as a mirror of how we and others of our generation lived in these years."

The magazine as a visual laboratory for experiments

The founders of Work in Progress regard *SELF SERVICE* as a "platform for all kinds of creative and expressive experiments, something that can give our other work wings."

"For us it is very important to take an experimental, independent approach to the exchange of ideas, and to have a passion for creative integrity. Even for fashion pages we oversee everything from the photo shoots to styling, layout design, typography and printing. In doing so we've continued to generate new ideas that distinguish us from preconceived notions of what's required to produce a magazine, and so the magazine has grown as an experimental medium. We are proud

to have been the ones to find raw talents who are now very influential people, and help them develop into global identities. The magazine is not about pushing ourselves to the fore, or just printing fashion pictures."

Editorial that brings a different look to the visuals

Ezra believes that words and meaning are as important to an image as the art direction in regard to giving life to the creative expression of an idea. It is the pair's strength in editorial and ideas that make their visuals and typography different from typical fashion magazines. Examples like using double exposure on ads for Helmut Lang and Dior Homme to show the similarity between the two campaigns, or putting Balenciaga designer Nicolas Ghesquière on the cover of the magazine to represent creative force in the fashion world, demonstrate how they have pursued their experimental editorial style and design techniques while remaining involved in the mainstream fashion world.

"Issue 13, 'The Influence,' published in 2000 was an important turning point for us," says Ezra. "It featured people from our own generation like Nicolas Ghesquière, Hedi Slimane, and Veronique Branquinho who have caused tremors in the conservative fashion culture of Paris, making it a highly significant issue."

Having interviewed more than 200 people from figures such as Miuccia Prada and Yves Saint Laurent to underground musicians and creatives, Ezra says that an important objective for *SELF SERVICE* is to project people behind the scenes as well as those in front. The magazine has developed extensive, highly stimulating relationships with leaders in music, art, fashion, literature, politics, the media and photography, further enriching the inspired landscape of the company. Collaborating with these individuals is in turn an experimental process generating enormous creativity, and it is this stimulating cycle that has brought them such success.

FIGURES LIBRE

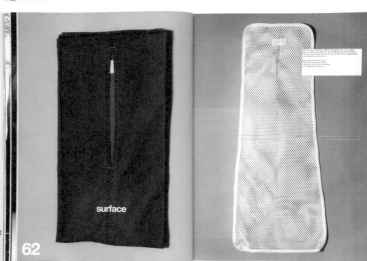

surface

vieilles
peaux

THIS SEASON IT'S HIP TO BE PRETTY AGAIN.

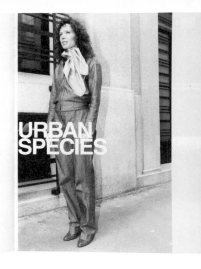

URBAN SPECIES

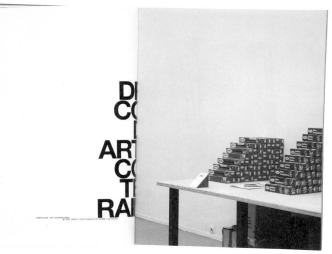

boys don't cry

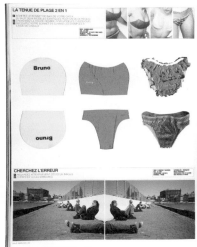

JE
M'AT
TA
CHE
AU
ROU
GE

photography by Paolo Roversi styling by Jane Hoss

ACHIE
VING
INSTANT
ELE
GANCE

photography by David Sims styling by Anna Cockburn

how does a young designer become established?

From the ever-maturing crop of young, creative thinkers, these collections are our pick, symbolic of the talent worth keeping an eye on. Their operations are still small enough so that their shows are personal statements and not gigantic categorical imperatives. With the fashion calendars becoming ever more crowded, it will be increasingly difficult for those starting out to catch the overwhelmed attentions of the exhausted fashion press. But they are not letting this force them into grasping blindly for gimmicks and hype. Rather, they are taking the time to experiment and find their unique personal style. Quiet revolutionaries, they are challenging the status quo simply by taking a self-reliant and pragmatic approach. Subtly undermining conventions, this integrity will make for a stronger legacy in the future.

now the ultimate way.

photography by Mario Sorrenti styling by Jane Hoss

I'VE BEEN A DDICTED TO GRAY CARDIG ANS SINCE H IGH SCHOOL

PHOTOGRAPHY BY TERRY RICHARDSON STYLING BY CAMILLE BIDAULT-WADDINGTON

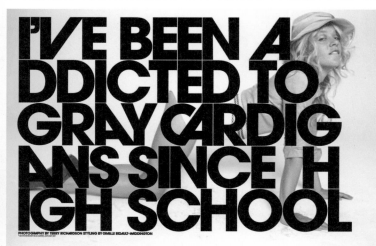

186

EXAGGERATE THE CLASSICS
TWIST THE BASICS
GIVE AN EDGE TO BEIGE

STABILIZE YOUR ENVIRONMENT

the smash

the obsessions

Calvin Klein Jeans

when is the timing right?

dressing
down
never
hurts

Photography by Richard Bush

THE TRUE HEROINES

Icons of personal style, champions of creative independence, defenders of the fashion faith, the women on these pages are some of the industry's true heroines. Collectively they have witnessed and played a role in some of the most revolutionary moments in fashion history. As representatives of the industry from all angles, be it editorial, public relations, or design, they have worked with all of "the great" mythic names, such as Avedon, Penn and Bourdin, reminding us of the value of apprenticeship and respect for the past. In their own careers there have been moments of great risk and all have stepped up to the challenge with strength, conviction, and above all, style. Most importantly, after a lifetime in fashion, their visions remain completely contemporary, their approaches creative and vital, their minds critical but completely wide open.

100 THINGS

by Suzanne Koller, Carina Frey, Marie Chaix and Patrick Li

INPR
OVISED
REFLECT
IONS

100 THINGS

by Suzanne Koller with Carina Frey, Marie Chaix, Nicolas Trembley

food for thought

STARS & STYLES

ASIA ARGENTO

conversation with Nicolas Ghesquière and Ezra Petronio　photographs by Suzanne Koller

Yesterday's International Bright Young Things may not be so young anymore, but the changing seasons have only added a shiny patina to their brilliance. We've clocked their progress these last few years and watched them go from zero to full speed ahead. And now that they're running with the fashion establishment, we're still cheering them on. We know it won't go to their heads: Their hard work is not for the sake of a quick ego trip, but a lifelong journey that's only just getting started. Shrewd and original thinkers, these are role models for a new wave of talent, not so much for the success they've achieved, but the way in which they've achieved it: On their own difficult terms. Véronique Branquinho, Raf Simons, Hussein Chalayan, Nicolas Ghesquière, Susan Cianciolo, Hedi Slimane, Viktor & Rolf, Véronique Leroy and Jeremy Scott. Even as larger-than-life fashion conglomerates recognize their talents and are fast turning them into house(hold) names, integrity, aptitude, spirit and enthusiasm remain their personal trademarks, which says more about them than any label or logo ever could. Commercial viability is pivotal for 2000 and beyond: Not only does it mean the ability to communicate on a universal level, it translates into the power to send more inspired intentions spinning into the ever-whirling fashion world. We're proud to say we're talking about our generation.

successful

Photography by Anuschka Blommers and Niels Schumm

STEFANO PILATI

CREATIVE DIRECTOR OF YVES SAINT LAURENT ON ELEGANCE AND SOPHISTICATION. ON UNDERSTANDING THE HISTORY OF A BRAND WHILE BRINGING IT INTO NEW TERRITORY.

PARIS, JANUARY 17TH 2006

the obsessions

N°5 CHANEL PARIS PARFUM

KIRSTEN WEARS A HAUTE COUTURE DRESS WITH

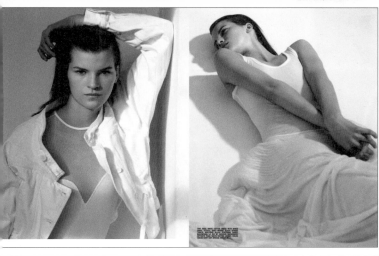

The obsessions

100 things

by Suzanne Keller, Carina Frey, Marie Chaix, Nicolas Trembley and Patrick Li.

personal insight
photography by Horst Diekgerdes
styling by Joe McKenna

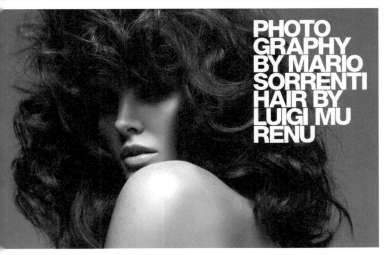

PHOTO
GRAPHY
BY MARIO
SORRENTI
HAIR BY
LUIGI MU
RENU

The obsessions

RUE
VIEILLE
DU TEMPLE

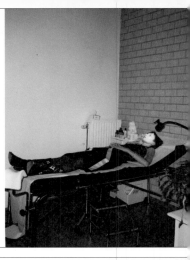

PHOTOGRAPHY BY JUERGEN TELLER STYLING BY CAMILLE BIDAULT-WADDINGTON

Photography by Juergen Teller / by Camille Bidault-Waddington / Hairdresser/Makeup

WANTED

Last issue we took the fierce initiative to celebrate the truly noble fashion heroes of our generation and began an ultra-special series of "Wanted Icons". No question about it, it was an awe-inspiring task for anyone. Its inauguration was blessed by Mr. Karl Lagerfeld, our first participant. This time the spotlight is on Mr. Yves Saint Laurent. What can we say? We reached out for the rainbow and found the pot of gold. Anticipation-overdrive kicked in... an interview with Yves Saint Laurent is like winning the lottery. There was always a slim possibility it might happen one day, but common sense tells you that the whole idea is just an ongoing figment of your imagination - a daydream to cherish. Then came the reality: a rendezvous with The Icon, a supremely humbling experience and one we couldn't wait to share. You know the facts and figures: his CV is tattooed onto every fashion disciple's heart. Headline news since the '60s, Yves Saint Laurent has always had the elusive appeal of legendary greats. We were lucky enough to catch a glimpse of his world. His press officer closed the door and left. Left us alone with Yves Saint Laurent. For the next sixty intense minutes we were face-to-face with him, looking into his benevolent eyes, breathing with him in his air space and absorbing every morsel of gentle integrity that fell from his lips. Here's what he said to us. **Interview by Ezra Petronio** **Photography by Jean-Baptiste Mondino**

It always takes a group of visionaries to change the way the system works, a group of people to boldly approach the status quo, take its reigns, and turn it in an unexpected direction. Catalysts of pop culture, spinners of style, unofficial trouble-shooters, they set an agenda of their own while the world waits to follow. Melanie Ward, Guido Palau, Katy England, Liz Goldwyn, Michel Botbol, Sarah, Joe McKenna, Steven Gan, Ginia Bellafante, Jefferson Hack, Eugene Souleiman, Matthias Vriens: In one way or another they have each infiltrated the establishment and are causing a revolution from within. Their new order has focused our attention to a younger generation of life's innovators, using their high-profile platforms to highlight the lesser known and worthy. They walk a fine line in their work, for as leaders they need to satisfy our need know, while satisfying the corporate chieftains who back their vision. Somehow these architects of insurrection have managed to do both, bringing the business and artistic communities into one worldview, without selling one out to the other. The casual and not so casual influence of these people is fascinating. While most of us are content with eagerly anticipating the future, know that it will clearly bear their stamp.

influential

Photography by / Anuschka Blommers and Niels Schumm

Model Leon Talley, Chanel Haute Couture, January 2002, Paris, photography by Juergen Teller

The art of planning ahead.

perceiving fashion fall/winter 2001

PERSONAL MATTERS SPRING 20 SUMMER 02

the return of the new

white is the great clarifier but always add a little touch of humor

photography by Richard Burbridge beauty editor: Marie Chaix

Haute but not haughty

photographs by Terry Richardson styling by Suzanne Koller

VALERIA GOLINO BY JUERGEN TELLER

100 things

by Suzanne Koller, Carina Frey and Marie Chaix

HOW SOON IS NOW

RIVOLI SISTER BY VANESSA BEECROFT

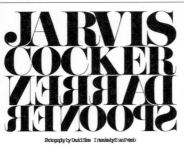

JARVIS COCKER DARREN SPOONER

Photography by David Sims Interview by Ezra Petronio

INDIS CRE TIONS EN NO IR

THE GREAT NEW HAIR

photography by Claudia McLellan, hair by Eugene Souleiman

STARS & STYLES POR TRAITS OF NEW YORK

PHOTOGRAPHY BY EZRA PETRONIO

The process of social documentation can be addictive, especially when it involves investigating our own environment. This time our curiosity took us and our circa 1970s Polaroid camera to New York City. In an attempt to document the creative forces, who share and shape our cultural landscape, we shot 150 New Yorkers in a little under six days. Not a pre-meditated grouping, but rather an organically unravelled network of people, acquaintances, friends, and friends of friends, 15-minute, one-on-one encounters, intimate and personal moments resulting in the revelation of each subject's inner beauty and stature, a subtle combination of genuine sincerity, truth, and an inevitable touch of glamour. A portfolio symbolic of the innumerable possible combinations that can occur at any given time, on any given day, random and yet revealing of the personalities and most certainly the spirit of New York. From a varied social mix, these pages comprise many of these people here come together for the first time on these pages. Unsuspecting therefore of the cultural continuity to which they all belong, they reflect individually and collectively the very essence of the city's creative soul.

L'ART IFICE DES LIGNES DRO IT ES

photography by Magnus Unnar styling by Bay Garnett

By Suzanne Koller, Carina Frey, Nicolas Trembley, Patrick Li, and Leela Petronio

INFLUENTIAL MEDIA

JONATHAN NEWHOUSE

CHAIRMAN OF CONDÉ NAST INTERNATIONAL LTD.

ON THE ROLE OF INSTINCT AND INTUITION IN SUCCESSFUL PUBLISHING, ON CORPORATE VISION, MANAGEMENT STYLE, AND LUXURY AS HUMAN NATURE.

At the helm of the second largest publishing group in the world, Jonathan Newhouse has successfully developed Condé Nast International Ltd. to include over 100 magazines in 15 countries around the globe, as well as 22 daily newspapers and 37 business journals throughout the United States. Under his leadership the company has also expanded its magazine influence into new markets such as China, Japan, Korea, Taiwan, Russia, South Africa, and Portugal, as well as various important and complementary sites on the World Wide Web. An independent thinker from an historical newspaper-publishing family, Jonathan is easily one of the great managers of our times. He is equally inspiring for his gracious yet hands-on management style, a capacity for detail as well as overview, and his marriage of high moral standards with market realities. Jonathan meets Ezra Petronio at Vogue House for a rare interview about the human necessity of luxury, long-term expectations, cultural dialogue, anticipating the desires of the readership, celebrity culture, finding talent and expression in unexpected places, the avant-garde versus the establishment, the self-indulgence of nostalgia, and most importantly, the eight golden rules to successful magazine management.

Conversation by Ezra Petronio Photography by Juergen Teller

This season, the obsessions have stretched to unknown horizons as we alphabetically illustrate our accessory instincts — hold the absurd, confuse the issues, discover the striped way and zoom in on the up. We have singled out the most instructive elements of style, concentrating on individual details without forgetting that, taken as a whole, these commandments of our most vivid fashion obsessions create a golden rule book of extraordinary seasonal style.

my abc

j

I TEND TO BE MORE MO DERN AND ART DECO

PHOTOGRAPHY BY KATJA RAHLWES STYLING BY SUZANNE KOLLER

MY ABC

ARCHITECTURAL THEORY

JACQUES HERZOG

ARCHITECT

ON TRANSCENDING THE BOUNDARIES OF ARCHITECTURAL THINKING. ON DEVELOPING A NETWORK OF KNOWLEDGE AND A BUILDING'S PLAYFULNESS WITH THE SKY.

ARDEN WOHL PHOTOG RAPHED BY TERRY RICHAR DSON STYLED BY BENJ AMIN ST URGILL

CLAUD IA SCH IFFER

PHOTOGRAPHED BY KATJA RAHLWES

UN LEASH SELF STYLED TH EA TRICS

foodforthought

B

THE SHAPE

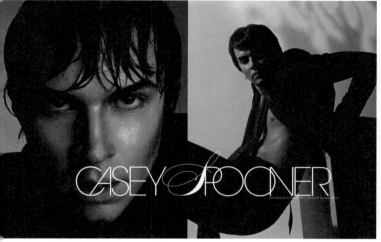

CASEY SPOONER

LESS HOK ESTY LE

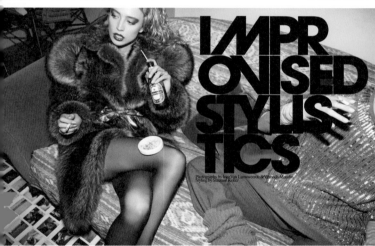

IMPR OVISED STYLIS TICS

the obsessions

FALL WINTER SUBJECTIVE UNDILUTED INTENTIONS

革新的クリエイティブエージェンシー、前衛的雑誌を展開

インディペンデントでありながら、この十年間、絶大な影響を与えてきたファッション＆カルチャー雑誌として知られる『SELF SERVICE』。その仕掛人はワーク・イン・プログレスの創設者パートナーであるエズラ・ペトロニオと、スザンヌ・コラーの２人だ。エズラはクリエイティビティのみならずビジネスセンスにも長けており、作品に魂を与えるスザンヌとの抜群の相性により、コムデギャルソン・パフューム、プラダ、ミュウミュウ、クロエなど、あらゆる一流ファッションブランドがクライアント

として名を連ねる。あくまでもクリエイティブエージェンシーとしての活動がメインであるが、雑誌はとても私的で芸術的な楽しみとして続けられている。

保守派から独立したメディアを構築

パリ、マレ地区にあるワーク・イン・プログレスのスタジオは、ミニマルなインテリアで統一され、ミーティングテーブルの上にもコンピューターと電話、インセンスキャンドル以外は何も置か

れていない。本棚には整頓された雑誌やアート本のコレクションがずらりと並び、その合間には彼らが手掛けたコムデギャルソンやプラダのパフュームが美しくディスプレイされている。彼らが『SELF SERVICE』を創刊させて12年が経つという。クリエイティブディレクターとしての立場から、エズラに話を聞いた。

「1995年に『SELF SERVICE』を創刊させたんだけど、その2年前にデザインエージェンシー、ワーク・イン・プログレスを設立しました。その頃のパリはアートやファッション、またその他の創造的表現が非常に保守的で、古い世代やメジャーの世界と、オルタナティブな世界との間に大きな溝があったんです。その一方で、若者の溢れんばかりのクリエイティブなエネルギーや才能を記録する、メディアや受け皿がまったく存在しなかった。当時まだコレットはないし、メールやインターネットもそれほど普及していなかったし。雑誌という媒体を通して、そんな行き場のない創造的エネルギーを表現するため、そして僕らの世代を描写するため、『SELF SERVICE』を立ち上げました。ヴィクトール＆ロルフやラフ・シモンズ、ダフトパンクまで、当時の僕ら世代にとってアップカミングだった、創造的世界の記録を試みたんです。ちょうどフランスのハウスミュージックシーンが盛り上がってきた時期でもありましたね。この12年間で、私たち自身が雑誌とともに成長してきたとも言えますし、ある意味で『SELF SERVICE』は我々や周りの人々の12年間の生き方や時代を、そのまま反映させているとも言えます」

実験を試みるビジュアルラボとしての雑誌

ワーク・イン・プログレスの創設者たちにとって、『SELF SERVICE』とは「さまざまな創造的表現的実験を試みることができるプラットフォームで、他の仕事を飛躍させるもの」だという。「私たちが一番大切にしているのは、常に実験的な独立した姿勢でアイデアを出し合うこと、そして創造性の品位を追求することです。ファッションページでも、撮影からスタイリング、レイアウトデザイン、タイポグラフィー、印刷に至るまで、既存の手法から切り離されたアイデアを持ち出すことで、"実験室"として

雑誌は発展してきました。また今、まさに影響力のあるクリエイターたちも、新人時代から発掘し、冒険的な新しい手法で紹介し、世界的に認知されるまでサポートしてきたと自負しています。単なるファッション写真を載せたり、我々のエゴを押し出すための媒体ではないのです」

編集ありきのアートディレクション

あるアイディアの創造的表現を生かそうとするアートディレクションと同じ比重で、ひとつのイメージにとって大事なことは、言葉と意味だと彼は言う。ありがちなファッション雑誌とは一線を画すヴィジュアルやタイポグラフィー使いも、編集やコンセプトが明確にあるからこそ成り立つ。例えば、誌内で掲載したディオールオムとヘルムートラングの広告ページをダブルエクスポージャーにして両者の広告の類似性を表現したり、ニコラス・ゲスキエール（バレンシアガのデザイナー）など、クリエイション側に立つ人物を表紙モデルに起用したりと、ファッション業界と密に関わりながら、その編集とデザイン技法では新しいことに挑戦する視点を追求してきた。

「2000年に発売した13号のテーマは"the influence(影響)"。僕らにとって特に重要な節目になった1冊です。ニコラス・ゲスキエール、エディ・スリマン、ヴェロニク・ブランキーノなど、保守的な社会に新しい波を生み出した同世代のクリエイターを集めた、示唆的な内容になりました」

ミウッチャ・プラダ やイヴ・サン・ローランなどの大物から、アングラ・ミュージシャン、クリエイターなど、200人以上のさまざまな人物と関わってきた『SELF SERVICE』。フロントに立つ人々だけでなく、裏方にいる人々にも焦点を当てることが非常に重要だと言う。雑誌を通じて、ファッションや音楽、アート、文学、政治に至るまで、各分野の先駆者と築いてきた刺激的な関係は、チームのクリエイティブ活動の原動力になっている。そして彼らとのコラボレーションが、さらに実験的でクリエイティブなものを生む。そんな刺激的なサイクルが、彼らを成功へと導いているのだ。

Work In Progress

Ezra Petronio and Suzanne Koller are the founders and creative directors of Work in Progress, a multi-disciplinary design company focusing on fashion, beauty, music, and art. Since 1993, they have collaborated with some of the industries leading references, including Comme des Garçons Parfums, Prada, Prada Fragrance & Beauty, Miu Miu, Chloé, Pucci, Nina Ricci and Rochas. Created with the intention of working independently within the confining structures of the advertising and publishing worlds, the company's projects range from visual identity, advertising, fragrance bottle design & packaging, to overall brand creative direction. The best and most comprehensive illustration of the design convictions of the company is *SELF SERVICE*, a biannual fashion and culture directional publication regarded as a leading reference for the fashion world.

ワーク・イン・プログレス

クリエイティブディレクターのエズラ・ペトロニオとスザンヌ・コラーによって1993年に設立されたデザインカンパニー。ファッション、ビューティー、音楽、アートを中心に多方面でデザイン活動を行い、コムデギャルソン・パフューム、プラダ、プラダ・フレグランス＆ビューティー、ミュウミュウ、クロエ、プッチ、ニナリッチ、ロシャスなど、多くの大手クライアントの仕事に携わる。広告や出版業界で独自の手法を提案し、単体のイメージヴィジュアルや広告、香水ボトルのデザインから、ブランド全体のクリエイティブディレクションまで、その仕事は幅広い。最も賞賛を浴びた仕事に、業界をリードする年2回発行のファッション＆カルチャー雑誌『SELF SERVICE』がある。

YORGO TLOUPAS

(CRASH, Intersection)

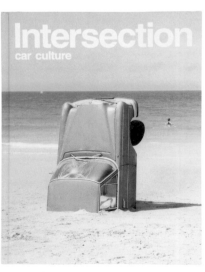

The way we exchange editing and design roles quite often is one of the things that makes the final product so interesting.

Intersection came as a breath of fresh air not only to those interested in car magazines, but to everyone in the magazine world. The magazine sets itself apart from the usual editorial style of its genre, and has a distinctive design aesthetic: the result no doubt of being edited by a car-loving art director.

Art direction for *CRASH*

The office of *Intersection* magazine lies in Old Street, East London, one of the British capital's main thoroughfares, leading in to Shoreditch, an area that changed dramatically from rundown former industrial area to centre of cutting edge creativity in the early '90s. *Intersection* shares a building with the headquarters of *Dazed and Confused*, one of the few British style magazines of the '90s to have survived from those 'good old days' of Shoreditch. Yorgo Tloupas plays a pivotal role in *Intersection*'s production: he is art director, co-publisher, and salesman all in one. Yorgo began working as a magazine art director at the relatively young age of 24, on French design culture magazine *CRASH*.

"After graduating from ESAG (Ecole Superieure d'Arts Graphiques, Paris) at the age of 21, I worked as a freelance graphic designer and art director. *CRASH* offered me the position of art director, saying I would have a lot of creative freedom as I'd be working for free. I worked from the second issue up to the twelfth issue, but when I began, the editors, Frank and Amelle, were also new to magazine production, so we tried out various different approaches and techniques and learnt a lot working there.

At the time I started working at *CRASH* in 1998, there weren't any French magazines that looked the way I wanted magazines to look. I knew there was an audience ready for a magazine that looked different to what else was around at the time, a lot of which were using a complex and multi-layered form of design. I wanted to produce something more minimal, in which the photos themselves took prominence, rather than the typography, and to create a template that would come across as more self effacing."

Layout that grew out of basic format

The design of *CRASH* had a big impact in the magazine world, and traces of its influence can be found in many publications today. Quitting *CRASH* after the twelfth issue, after working as a freelance art director for various high profile clients and art directing a free magazine named *Magazine* for French book retailer OFR, Yorgo decided to co-found a new publication with writer and editor Dan Ross, a magazine that would offer a fresh perspective on car culture – in its visual expression, locations, use of models, and even the angles at which cars were shown. Thus in 2001 *Intersection* was born.

"My favourite magazine is not necessarily one with a great design or visual aspect. I am more interested in engaging subject matter and the way in which the subject is handled. Take *Vanity Fair* for example: the art direction is not always that great, but they have a very interesting way of presenting the stories.

The reason I started this magazine is, apart from the obvious – the fact that I like cars, that I wanted to make a specialist magazine by choosing a very precise subject and developing and expanding from there; observing the culture – music, design, art, fashion – surrounding the subject.

As far as the visual aspect is concerned, of course we try to make it feel luxurious and to convey that it's a well thought out product, but for me, the most important thing is that we try to make *Intersection* accessible and easy to read, with headlines standing first and columns that are not too wide so that when people flick through the magazine in a news agent they can quickly see what it's about. The basic format is important to us

Juggling both editorial and design

Intersection is pioneering in the world of car magazines in that it has expanded the subject by tapping into the cultural and fashion aspects relevant to the genre. Right from the start I had a premonition that it would be an awesome magazine, and I remember buying two copies of the first issue, which had a hard cover.

"I'm not just the art director," says Yorgo, "I write articles, do illustrations and design the map – a crucial element of the magazine. I even test drive some of the cars. Dan Ross, the editor of *Intersection*, mainly writes and edits the magazine, but also takes a strong interest in the visual aspect, suggesting design ideas for fashion stories and covers. The way we exchange editing and design roles quite often is one of the things that makes the final product so interesting."

A lot of people in the magazine industry are constantly on the go, and Yorgo is no exception. When I visited he was bustling about: it was like watching myself. A lover of all things mechanical, he commutes on his treasured bicycle, and I must say I rather liked his active, enthusiastic style.

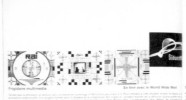

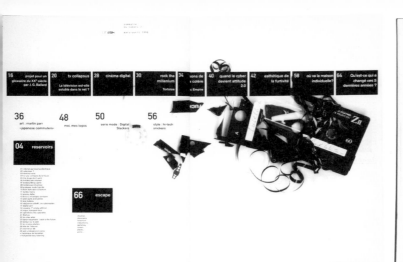

cinéma digital

Les contemporains

Le pionnier

Bazar digital

Projections

esthétique de la furtivité

Esthetique de la furtivité, origines et formes

Un concept postmoderne

MARTIN PARR
METRO PICTURES

JAPANESE COMMUTERS
PHOTOS MARTIN PARR

où va la maison individuelle ?

Que reste-t-il de l'idée de Maison aujourd'hui ? Que deviennent l'hospitalité et la chaleur domestique à l'ère des nouvelles technologies? Quelle sera la maison du futur? Derrière ces questions innocentes se cache l'une des interrogations existentielles relevant pour les uns d'une angoisse très "fin de siècle", pour les autres d'un espoir "début de millénaire".

Software et espace public

Relectures postmodernes

Couch potator et house video

reservoirs

01 Web guerilla
Les Guerilla Girls sévissent sur le Net

02 Décès de Tamagotchis

03 Les cartes d'Alphaworld
Les communautés virtuelles grossissent aussi

04 Hologramme amoureux
Idoru de William Gibson

05 Videorewrite
Synchronisation labiale de synthèse

dossier

l'esthétique 64 bits

dossier

la fin
du travail

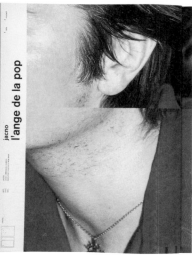

jacno
l'ange de la pop

Depuis deux décennies Jacno incarne l'une des figures les plus inclassables de la scène française. *La part des anges* signe sa plus récente incarnation.

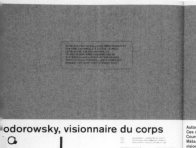

Jodorowsky, visionnaire du corps

Autour de l'imaginaire du corps, une rencontre avec le génial Jodorowsky s'imposait. Ces derniers mois ont vu paraître deux œuvres majeures : le tome final du "Cœur Couronné" (le Fou de la Sorbonne), de Mœbius et le tome 5 de "La Caste des Méta-barons". Jodorowsky est certainement le scénariste de bande dessinée dont les visions cosmiques pourraient bien illuminer les Terriens que nous sommes.

Le cœur désintégré

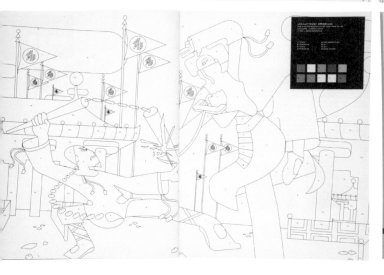

fela
music is the weapon
of the future

reservoirs

01   Iridium au
      Kosovo

Quand les réfugiés deviennent
relais publicitaires

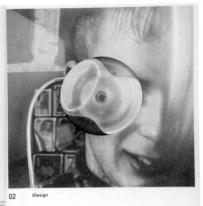

02   iDesign

Plastique planétaire

polnareflexion

french electr- onica

Le syndrome de Peter Pan
L'espace, le cosmos, la technologie, le réseau des réseaux, les mutations génétiques,
les entrailles de la machine... Voilà autant de thèmes souvent associés à l'univers des
musiciens électroniques. Depuis l'apogée de leurs ancêtres allemands des années 70 (la
barbe fleurie, le visage embué sous les effluves de cannabis, face au mur d'une montagne de synthétiseurs), les technophiles ont bien changé. La période de
glorification de la machine vit sans doute ses derniers jours, et seul les groupes un peu
nostalgiques continuent à brandir l'étendard de la technologie triomphante.
Chez les jeunes artistes français que nous avons choisi ici, on versera plutôt du côté
cinéma classique, d'une certaine poésie désuète, de la télé des seventies et du
consumérisme de masse. Quelque part entre Barbapapa, Smarties, le jazz de papa,
Cassavetes, Polnareff, Chapi-Chapo et autres enfantillages... nous entrons heureusement
dans l'ère insolente de l'electro multi-sources...

Cosmo Vitelli   Alex Gopher

un monde sans machine

nature 2000

Et si l'avenir de la machine était sa disparition,
sa dissolution dans un monde de plus en plus
fluide ? Et s'il fallait se débarrasser de la
fascination technologique pour ne pas être
colonisé par la nation-gédéon ? Notre époque
signe l'adieu aux machines. Bon vent, vive
la dématérialisation joyeuse, et faisons ce
stop du côté d'une éco-technologie éclairée
à construire. De toute façon, les ordinateurs
meurent aussi... Et n'oublions jamais que le
futur est sauvage, forcément...

Pour en finir avec les cyber- gédéons

Dans son pamphlet intitulé «Vivre et penser
comme des porcs», le mathématicien
et philosophe Gilles Châtelet instruit le procès
au vitriol du technopopulisme qui gangrène
aujourd'hui les démocraties-marchés.

mode 2000
défilé d'attitudes

bless

hussein chalayar

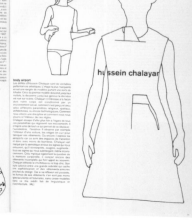

/99

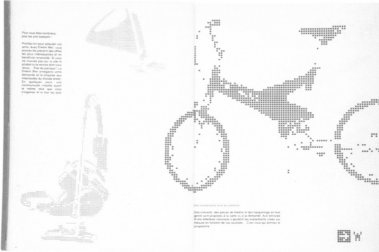

watch out
the house !

crash
NINETY NINE

01 *Génération Y*

Nous sommes dans la glisse sous toutes ses formes, dans l'esquive d'une façon générale plutôt que dans l'antique confrontation de la mythologie soixante-huitarde. Aucune expérience historique collective n'a fait naître pour notre génération de sentiment identitaire. Nous sommes une tribu avec son propre cryptage. La/les générations d'aujourd'hui sont satellisés en réseaux, fragmentées en niches. Nous sommes cette génération sans unité.

Il n'est plus question de se confronter au système mais de trouver en lui les failles et les lignes de fuite. De sampler et de surfer les systèmes ambiants, de trouver dans les anciennes organisations pyra-midales les combinatoires réticulaires et les agencements actifs. La génération X de Coupland est la dernière qui a vécu la vacance du travail et la crise d'activité. De la grunge attitude à la génération homestudio : nous sommes cette génération, invisible en termes d'identité et omniprésente en termes d'activité, de connectiques. Agrégats soniques, stylistiques, digitaux, enfants de l'interface, où musique/mode/digitale attitude/flux urbains sont un même bloc, et constitue notre bain amniotique.

Le global digital a aplati toute provenance, nous sommes en temps réel et en connexions multiples.

Nous sommes la première génération de cette globalité nouvelle. (FP)

dirk seider
compost

richesse mondiale

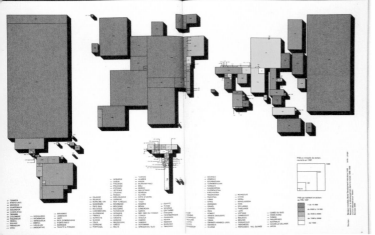

love office

Le meilleur moyen de se prémunir de tous problèmes liés au harcèlement sexuel est assurément la buro cam. Cousine de la web cam associée à l'univers du travail, souvent cadrée en dessous de la ceinture pour saisir tous les mouvements suspects, elle offre ainsi une nouvelle perspective sur l'univers du travail. Mais encore pour récuser Marcuse qui voulait qu'entre travail et plaisir, la société industrielle nous oblige à choisir, redécouvrez d'urgence le bureau comme lieu de plaisir.

Afin de précipiter le passage vers la société numérique, militez pour le cybernaturisme au bureau, vivez nu sur le lieu de travail en visio conférence dans le glanding et la plus grande débauche.

A l'heure du bureau virtuel et de la cyber secrétaire, relégué au plan des antiquités et désormais inutile, le bureau n'est plus qu'un lieu de fantasmes.

Dans la société digitale, son futur est certainement d'être reconverti du coté de la pornographie.

Et le bureau deviendra la maison close de la société cybernétique. Un jour aussi, il fermera. En attendant cette apocalypse bureautique imminente, profitez de ce qu'il reste du mobilier.

el

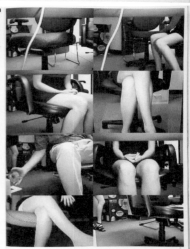

la coccinelle,
le monstre,
la grotte et l'église
photographies camille vivier

Ufo

After his 021C car for Ford, the sky was the limit. Has Marc Newson's Kelvin 40 invented the concept jet?

Photography: Alexis Armanet

Can you kick it?

The Hummer H3T – designed in collaboration with Nike – should come with steel toecaps...

Dad

Family-friendly vehicles which parents can feel cool driving are few and far between. A couple of MPV concepts going into production may help mum and dad forget.

Text Guy Bird

Restrained design

They're belting out new designs faster than you can snap a buckle shot

Text Sarah AlKhalos

Slick-up truck

Japan adds insult to injury by making their American pick-ups beautiful as well as big

Text Guy Bird

Road runner

Last time we heard of a Ford Bronco, it was white and chased by cops live on TV

A Van-time

Spot the difference

Fat cars

Half of America might be on the Atkins Diet but not these cars

1980

Back to the Future

It may be the start of a decade synonymous with greed, selfishness and excess but, with the exception of a new Roller, the cars shown in 1980 are a pretty humble bunch – welcome Mini Metro and Fiat Panda

Walk it

Photography Robe Rodriguez
Coordination Shirley Amaldry

Work it

Photography Jack Weizmann
Styling Shirley Amaldry

Bus'

Busta Rhymes selects his cars as carefully as his beats. He has to make sure each one's a hit.

PHOTOGRAPHY SPIROS POLITIS
INTERVIEW GUY BIRD

stop and star search

Don't be disarmed by British actress Sienna Guillory's sensible Saab

PHOTOGRAPHY DONALD MILNE
INTERVIEW SKYE SHERWIN

Alu-minium body

Photography Vanina Sorrenti
Styling Mattias Karlsson

BELT UP

**PHOTOGRAPHY
SASHA EISENMAN
STYLING
VANESSA MOORE**

'OLD SCHOOLERS COMPARE IT TO FISHING: A LOT OF WAITING AROUND, BUT WHEN A CATCH IS MADE, AN INCOMPARABLE THRILL'

'WHENEVER HE TURNED AROUND I'D WHACK IT IN FOR A FEW STROKES, AND THEN PULL OUT. HE NEVER CAUGHT ME AND IT DROVE HER WILD'

"THE DRIVER WAS LIKE: 'DO YOU NEED TO GO TO THE HOSPITAL?' AND I SAID: 'NO, THANKS, I HAVE TO GO DO A READING'"

SAN FRANCISCO AUTHOR **JT LEROY** PUTS IN A TRANSCONTINENTAL CALL TO NEW YORK ACTOR **LEO FITZPATRICK** TO CATCH UP AFTER THEY WERE DUE TO MEET AT A READING OF JT'S WORK.
PHOTOGRAPHY JORDAN BENNETT

WILD ONES
**PHOTOGRAPHY
NICK CLEMENTS
STYLING
LINCOLN JACOBS**

MKI

**PHOTOGRAPHY
BEN KELWAY
STYLING
THOM MURPHY**

AIR RACING IN RENO

FERRARICKSHAW

BEAUTY AND THE BEAST

PHOTOGRAPHY LAETITIA NEGRE
STYLING ANNA BURNS

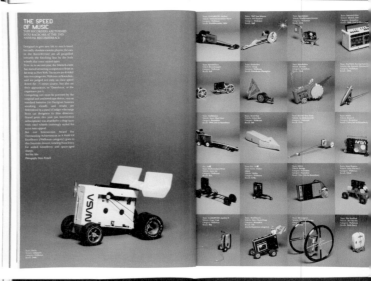

THE SPEED OF MUSIC

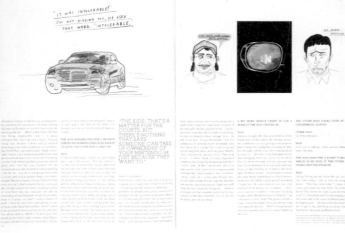

SHORT CUTS

"THE KIDS, THAT'S A MATTER FOR THE COURTS, BUT THERE'S NOTHING THAT SAYS SOMEONE CAN TAKE UP OWNERSHIP OF YOUR NINTENDO 64 JUST BECAUSE THEY WANT TO"

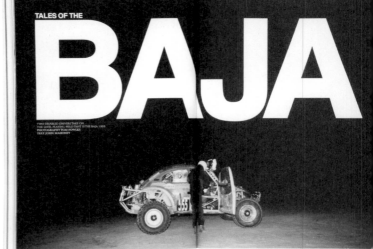

TALES OF THE

BAJA

THE COLLECTOR

"I'VE ALWAYS LIKED PURPOSEFUL THINGS. THINGS THAT ARE DESIGNED NOT JUST TO BE DECORATIVE"

EXK 6

RISING DAMP

PHOTOGRAPHY SPIROS POLITIS
STYLING SHAZY THOMAS

HOW RAIN MADE SANTA POD'S ANNUAL FLAME & THUNDER SPECIAL A SLOW BURNER

SEARCH
CARCHITECTURE

NISSAN'S CAR DESIGN REVIVAL IS MIRRORED BY ITS APPROACH TO CORPORATE ARCHITECTURE. INTERSECTION VISITED ITS LATEST LONDON AND TOKYO STRUCTURES.

IN POD WE TRUST

ICE
LAND

SHOWFFEURS

LAST
RIDES

In Bangkok, in the absence of an official ambulance service, Buddhist charities patrol the streets. Carrying those they find to the morgue or the hospital, the drivers of Ruemkatanyu spend their nights bringing in the dead and searching out the living

Photography
Alex Cayley
at Creative Exchange Agency

Styling
Maria Serra

Models
Heidi Klum at IMG and **Johnny Zander** at DNA New York

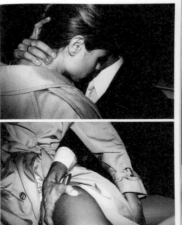

'I'd been having dinner with Monsieur and Madame Ungaro. I was about to call a taxi when he announced: "You're going home by car!" I didn't want him to go out of his way. He insisted: "No, you don't understand," and gave me a set of keys'

118 OLD STREET

THE BEST
KEBAB & FRIED CHICKEN

21

Intersection
CONTENTS

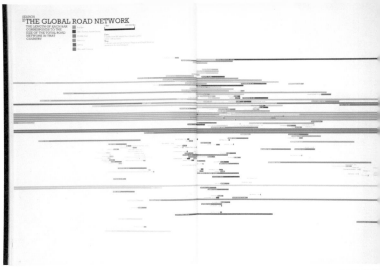

SEARCH
THE GLOBAL ROAD NETWORK
THE LENGTH OF EACH BAR CORRESPONDS TO THE SIZE OF THE TOTAL ROAD NETWORK IN THAT COUNTRY

SEARCH
BACK TO THE FUTURE

1958

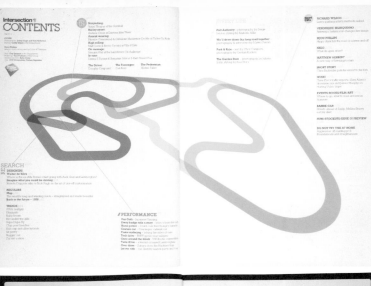

GOING BACK IN TIME FURTHER THAN EVER BEFORE, INTERSECTION'S TIME MACHINE DISCOVERS A COLD WORLD, OBSESSED WITH NUCLEAR TESTING, THE SPACE RACE, AND ROCK AND ROLL. SEE WHAT THE CARS LOOKED LIKE

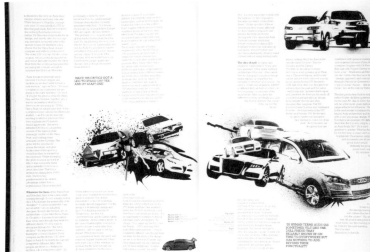

VAN GOTH

1983
WE'LL DRIVE DOWN THIS LONG ROAD TOGETHER

WHY CHANGE YOUR CAR EVERY THREE YEARS WHEN YOU CAN GROW OLD WITH THE ONE YOU LOVE? INTERSECTION CELEBRATES THOSE WHO CHOOSE AUTOMOTIVE MONOGAMY

2003

PARK & RIDE

Dutch experiments in social design led to the establishment of a new type of red light district – the drive-in brothel

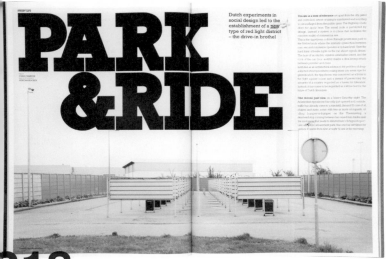

'Post-crash my assistant said: 'You're crying about your car! I bet you wouldn't cry if anything happened to us!'

www.scottjenkins.net
www.samjenkins.net

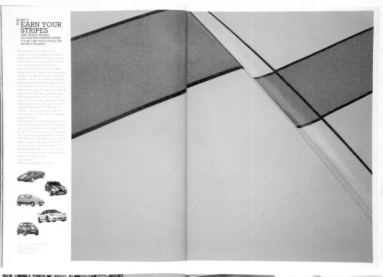

EARN YOUR STRIPES
LIKE SPEED HOLES,
GO-FASTER STRIPES MAKE
YOUR CAR THAT LITTLE BIT
MORE DYNAMIC

HAPPY ANNIVERSARY?
AS FORD AND VAUXHALL CELEBRATE 100 YEARS IN BUSINESS
WE ASK IF MARKETING A GLORIOUS PAST REFLECTS
ANXIETY ABOUT THE FUTURE

OIL SLICK
GOOD ENOUGH FOR A
FASHION BRAND AND A FILM
STAR, DIESEL IS NO LONGER A
DIRTY WORD WHEN IT COMES
TO LUXURY CARS

PERFORMANCE
DOG TOWN AND Z CAR
AFTER REALISING HOW BIG A DOG WE
COULD FIT IN THE XL-1, WE DECIDED TO
CONTINUE OUR DOG TEST.
OUR NEXT KENNEL,
THE NISSAN 350Z COUPE

THE MAN WITH BLOOD ON HIS WHEELS

'At 14, he would drive
himself to school in a
Porsche and order his
bodyguards to seize a
car belonging to the
families of fellow pupils
if he liked the look of it'

'The invasion of Kuwait
was an added bonus'

Music

'You'd just knock
on the door and
the band would
say 'Come on in''

Pamela Des Barres
**Rocking
on the road**

Trevor Jackson
**Why don't they
make cars ugly
like they used to?**

The Mix

Zongamin
Fantasy race mix

THE DRIVER
STEPHEN FRY

FACE ON

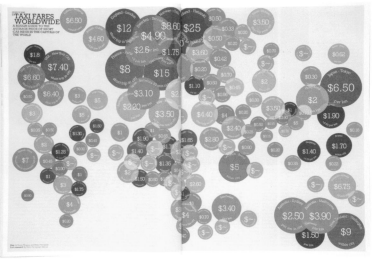

TAXI FARES WORLDWIDE
A ROUGH GUIDE TO THE AVERAGE PRICE OF SHORT CAB RIDES IN THE CAPITALS OF THE WORLD

DAY ON EARTH

If there's one thing you'll find in every town on earth, it's someone who'll give you a ride. But who picks you up, what tales they have to tell and what happens to you in the back – well, that's another story

BEIRUT · LEBANON

In the dusty desolation of southern Zimbabwe, thousands attempt to cross illegally into South Africa. Waiting to deliver, rob or rape them are the guns gangs, mercenary taxi drivers whose living comes from smuggling the starving and desperate out of their collapsing homeland

THE BRIDGE

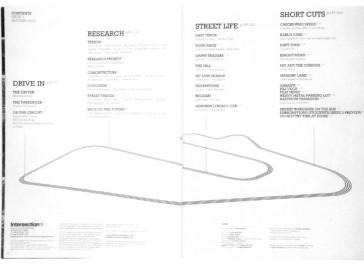

CONTENTS

Intersection

GOODWOOD FESTIVAL OF SPEED

LE MANS

RE SEARCH

THE SHAPE OF CARS TO COME

ASTON ZAGATO

OLD TO THE NEW

SEARCH

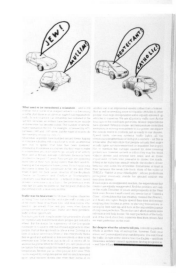

LIGHT CLUSTERS

PEDESTRIAN SAFETY

IN FLIGHT ENTERTAINMENT

GO INVADE

THE HILL

THE PIKES PEAK HILL CLIMB IS ONE OF THE LAST GREAT RACES LEFT IN AMERICA. A THROWBACK TO A TIME WHEN COLORADO STILL FELT LIKE A FRONTIER. ITS APPEAL GROWS WITH EACH PASSING YEAR THAT IT STAYS THE SAME

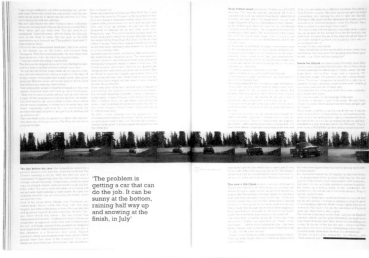

'The problem is getting a car that can do the job. It can be sunny at the bottom, raining half way up and snowing at the finish, in July'

CHICKS WHO SPEED

K

ARL'S CARS

KARL LAGERFELD IS SYNONYMOUS WITH HIGH FASHION LUXURY, TASTE AND SOPHISTICATION. INTERSECTION AUDITS HIS PERSONAL FLEET AND FINDS GOLF CARTS AND A DISCO VAN UNACCOUNTED FOR

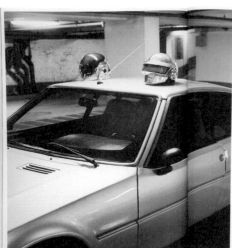

FRENCH MODERN CLASSIC
FOR SALE
THREE FRONT SEATS, TWO CARELESS OWNERS GOOD BODYWORK, ENGINE NEEDS ATTENTION

REASON FOR SALE: NEGLECT ALL OFFERS CONSIDERED

INTERSECTION ACCEPTS ITS FIRST CLASSIFIED AD - DAFT PUNK'S RARE 1979 MATRA SIMCA BAGHEERA. WE FIND OUT WHERE THE OWNERS HAVE BEEN WHILST THEIR TECHNOSTALGIC TOY LANGUISHED IN A PARIS CAR PARK FOR TWO YEARS

PT CRUISER GOLF BUGGY
PALM SPRINGS, USA
2001

BACK TO THE FUTURE

IN LOOKING BACKWARDS
FORWARD THINKING?
TEXT UMA JONES

GUCCI CADDY

TEXT
EMMA E FORREST
PHOTOGRAPHY
DANIEL STIER

ON THE RUN

LAGOS

MOTOR CITY
LAGOS NIGERIA
TEXT MUW
WILLIAMS

1. CUTTING OFF CIRCULATION

MOTOR CITY CONE

PAUL TAFFA WAS OFTEN TO BE SEEN STANDING IN THE STREET WITH HIS BULLWHIP-WIELDING TROOPS, SUPERVISING THE MEN UNFURLING THEIR WEAPONS ON TERRIFIED DRIVERS

THE CHEAP MOBILES DON'T COME SOON THEN LAGOS HAS LITTLE CHANCE OF MAKING FROM ITS TRAFFIC NIGHTMARE. IN ALL COMMUNICATION, SOCIAL OR BUSINESS, MUST TAKE PLACE FACE TO FACE

III. CALL A FRIEND

THE BEGINNING
OF THE ROAD
OR ANOTHER

MY OTHER CAR IS
A GIANT ROBOT

編集とデザインの役割に境目がない点が
この雑誌を面白くしているのかもしれませんね

　『Intersection』の登場は、クルマ雑誌に興味を持つ人だけでなく、雑誌に関わる全ての人間を驚かせた。編集手法に独自の考えがあり、デザインが斬新だったからだ。クルマ好きのアートディレクターが自ら編集に関わったことから生まれた、特別な結果だと言える。

『CRASH』のアートディレクション

　そのオフィスは東ロンドンのオールドストリート沿いにあった。ロンドンを代表する大通りの一つで、ショーディッチ地区へとまたがっている。かつて寂れた工業地域だったこの場所は、90年代初頭からクリエイターが集まる最先端エリアとして大きな変貌を遂げた。そんな絶頂期に創刊された英国カルチャー誌の数少ない成功例『Dazed and Confused』と同じビルに、『Intersection』の拠点がある。雑誌の中心的存在であるヨルゴ・トゥルーパスは共同発行人、アートディレクター、営業として1人で何役をもこなしている。そんな彼の雑誌キャリアは、弱冠24歳で『CRASH』のアートディレクターに就任したことから始まったという。

　「21歳でESAG（パリ美術学校）を卒業し、フリーランスでデザインの仕事をしていました。雑誌『CRASH』からの提案は、タダ働きではあるけど、アートディレクターとしてやりたいことをやらせてもらえるというポジション。2号目から12号目まで関わったんだけど、始めた頃は編集者のフランクとアーメルも雑誌作りはまったくの初心者で、みんなで試行錯誤しながら、いろいろ学びました。ちょうど『CRASH』のデザインを始めた1998年頃のフランスには、自分にとって理想的な雑誌は見当たらなかった。レイヤーを重ねたギミックなものが多かったり、フォントが凝りすぎていたり。だから『CRASH』ではミニマルなフォーマットを作って、タイポグラフィーよりも写真自体を生かした、控えめなデザインを心掛けたんです」

基本フォーマットから派生したレイアウト

　『CRASH』のデザインは雑誌界に明確なインパクトを残し、今もさまざまな雑誌でその影響を見ることができる。12号目で『CRASH』を離れたヨルゴは、その後フランスのアート系書店OFRのフリーペーパー『Magazine』のアートディレクションを担当するなど、幅広く活動を続ける。そして2001年に編集者兼ライターであるダン・ロスとともに、自らが共同発行人になり『Intersection』を創刊。ヴィジュアル表現やロケ場所、モデルの扱い、クルマを見せるアングルまでにも新しさを感じさせた。

　「僕の好きな雑誌は、必ずしもデザインやヴィジュアルがよいものとは限りません。それよりも扱う題材が面白くなければいけないし、その編集方法の方が気になります。例えば『Vanity Fair』のアートディレクションは必ずしもよいとは思いませんが、記事の見せ方が非常に興味深いのです。

　『Intersection』を始めた理由は、もちろん自分がクルマ好きなことは言うまでもありませんが、クルマという専門的な題材にフォーカスし、そこから派生した音楽、デザイン、アート、ファッションなどのカルチャーを全般的に扱う雑誌を作ってみたかったからです。もちろん雑誌のヴィジュアル面で、高級感や完成度も求めていますが、一番気を遣っているのは読みやすさと親しみやすさ。『Intersection』は街角の新聞スタンドなどでも売っているから、そこで立ち読みして、すぐに内容を理解できるようにしたかった。だからどんなアレンジを加えたデザインでも、記事の最初に見出しを付けたり、読みやすい欄の幅を守るなど、基本のフォーマットを大事にしています」

編集とデザイン、両方に関わる作り方

　クルマの専門誌でありながら、ここまで広くファッションやカルチャーに膨らませた雑誌というのは世界で初めてだろう。当初からすごい雑誌になる予感があり、書籍みたいなハードカバーの創刊0号を2冊買ったことを覚えている。

　「この雑誌で僕はアートディレクターとしてだけでなく、記事も書くし、イラストも描く。クルマの試運転もするし、誌面の重要なイメージ素材である地図もデザインしている。本当にあらゆることをします。同時にダン・ロスもファッションページやカバーのデザインアイデアを提案することもある。編集とデザインの役割に境目がない点が、この雑誌を面白くしているのかもしれませんね」

　雑誌に関わる人にはせっかちな人が多い。取材に行くと彼もせわしなく動いていた。その姿は自分を見るようだった。メカ好きで自慢の自転車で通勤しているらしく、アクティブなスタイルに好感を持った。

Yorgo Tloupas

Born 1974 in Paris, from a Greek sculptor father and a French-Italian art teacher mother. Graduated from the Paris art school ESAG in 1996. Tloupas has worked as art director and designer of catalogues and advertising for a great many clients including Yves Saint Laurent, Shu Uemura, Lacoste, and Kenzo. He acted as art director of issues 2 through 12 of the French culture magazine *CRASH* in 1998, designing the logo and original layout, and thereafter of the free paper *Magazine* published by the Paris art bookshop OFR. In 2001, with Dan Ross and Rankin from *Dazed & Confused*, he launched the car culture magazine *Intersection*, acting as art director and co-publisher. He is currently based in London, expanding his work to a broad range of magazines and advertising.

ヨルゴ・トゥルーパス

1974 年パリにて、ギリシア人彫刻家の父と、フランス系イタリア人美術教師の母の間に生まれる。1996 年パリの美術学校 ESAG 卒業。アートディレクター・デザイナーとして、イヴ・サン・ローラン、シュウ・ウエムラ、ラコステ、ケンゾー等多数のクライアントのカタログや広告を手掛ける。1998 年にはフランスのカルチャー雑誌『CRASH』の 2 〜 12 号までのロゴやレイアウトのデザイン・アートディレクションを、その後パリのアートブックショップ OFR が発行するフリーペーパー『Magazine』のアートディレクションを担当。2001 年に車をテーマにした雑誌『Intersection』を『Dazed & Confused』のダン・ロスとランキンの二人と共に立ち上げ、アートディレクター兼発行人として活躍。現在ロンドンを拠点に、雑誌や広告の仕事を幅広く展開している。

雑誌デザインの潮流を変えた10人

2007年11月6日 初版第1刷発行
2008年11月5日 初版第2刷発行

著者　藤本やすし（CAP）

デザイン　嶋田典彦（CAP）
　　　　　野村まさひこ
撮影　　　武藤彩
　　　　　藤牧徹也
　　　　　島田洋平
　　　　　Ami Sioux
　　　　　Takashi Kamei
　　　　　Judith van IJken
執筆　　　大澤佑介（Rocket Company*/RCKT）
　　　　　工藤健士（Rocket Company*/RCKT）
　　　　　武藤彩
　　　　　寺島彩子
翻訳　　　パメラ・三木
編集　　　高橋かおる
協力　　　大山ゆかり（Rocket Company*/RCKT）
　　　　　TMDC（Tokyo Magazine Design Club）

発行人　　三芳伸吾
発行元　　ピエ・ブックス
　　　　　〒170-0005 東京都豊島区南大塚 2-32-4
　　　　　編集 TEL：03-5395-4820　FAX：03-5395-4821
　　　　　営業 TEL：03-5395-4811　FAX：03-5395-4812
　　　　　http://www.piebooks.com
　　　　　e-mail：editor@piebooks.com
　　　　　sales@piebooks.com

印刷・製本　株式会社サンニチ印刷